SCIENCE AND SOCIAL ACTION

SCIENCE AND SOCIAL ACTION

*Josiah Mason Lectures
delivered at the
University of Birmingham*

BY

W. J. H. SPROTT

Professor of Psychology at the
University of Nottingham

WATTS & CO

LONDON

First published 1954
Reprinted 1961

Made and printed by offset in Great Britain by William Clowes and Sons, Limited, London and Beccles, and published by C. A. Watts and Co Ltd, 39 Parker Street, London, W.C.2

Contents

Preface

WHEN I received the invitation to deliver the Josiah Mason Memorial Lectures at Birmingham in 1953 I gathered that I was invited to discuss current theoretical problems in the field of sociology. My predecessors were distinguished anthropologists and archæologists; they had dealt in the main with the "simpler peoples" or with the remote past. I took it to be my own task to say something about the more complex fields of research in modern large-scale societies. In these fields there is no accepted doctrine to expound and I had no disclosures to make about unfamiliar ways of life. I ventured, therefore, to raise theoretical questions which interested me personally and which I believe to be of importance to the student of social science. I took the opportunity of placing my own difficulties before the audience, and for this reason the lectures are published almost in their original form.

In the first four and in the last two I have attempted to discuss general theoretical issues. In the fifth and sixth I turned to two specific fields of inquiry which happened to be uppermost in my mind at the time.

It was my intention to provoke discussion, and I should like to take this opportunity to thank the staff and students of the Department of Commerce and Social Science at Birmingham University for the way they responded with criticism and encouragement. I should like particularly to express my gratitude to Professor Charles Madge for his unfailing kindness and support. I venture to hope that the discussion will be continued by those who are good enough to read the lectures in printed form.

W. J. H. S.

January, 1954

CHAPTER I

The Nature of Social Action

I UNDERSTAND that the intention of those who founded this series of lectures in memory of Josiah Mason was to encourage what is generally known as the scientific study of society. Man has systematically pursued the study of his physical environment from those early beginnings with agriculture, stockbreeding, textiles, and ceramics, so brilliantly described by one of my distinguished predecessors, Professor Gordon Childe, in his *Man Makes Himself*,[1] down to the latest developments in physics, chemistry, and technology, which have given man a considerable command over the forces of Nature. The conventional view is that more recently—some would say with the French Encyclopædists, others would say with the establishment of the first Psychological Laboratory in Leipzig by Wundt in 1875— man began the systematic study of himself. More recently still—in fact, in our own age—he has taken seriously the Comtian thesis that the final, crowning scientific discipline is the systematic study of the social order of which he is a constituent. Such is the conventional view, and there is no doubt something in it.

Of course a great deal is left out of account. We omit all reference to Indian psychology and to the Arthasāstra of Kautilya, an impressive work on government; we leave out of account the psychology of Plato and the sociology of Aristotle; we forget the writings of Ibn Khaldun in the fifteenth century, and the sociological and

[1] Thinker's Library (Watts, 1951).

1

psychological theories of the Schoolmen. They were not, we say, systematic. They were not " scientific." They were governed by the spirit of their age and culture. We, it is presumed, are free of such trammels ; we can view ourselves and our social environment dispassionately. This I believe to be mistaken. It is true, as I shall suggest in the third chapter, that our ways of thinking about society are in a sense more *explicitly* scientific ; we demand that certain standards of evidence shall be met; we apply statistical calculations; we compare a group with certain characteristics—say, the delinquency of all its members—with a group alike in many features but the members of which are not delinquent, so as to see in what further respects the two groups differ. This is the kind of thing we have in mind when we talk about the " scientific " study of society.

To leave the matter there, however, seems to me to savour too much of the notion of the " pure scientist," divorced from the practical concerns of everyday life, turning his gaze first upon the heavens over Babylon ; then, while in his bath, apprehending the principles of mechanics ; then, crowned with the steeple hat of a necromancer, unravelling chemical mixtures ; then, surrounded with expensive apparatus, discovering the ultimate constituents of matter ; then, armed with tests and apparatus, finding out the nature of human nature, and now, finally, with a sheaf of questionnaires and a Hollerith machine, studying society. Such a picture is, of course, absurd ; but it is not absurd because chemists do not wear steeple hats ; it is absurd because it portrays the scientist as a man apart ; it hints at "science" as a special way of thinking and looking which is quite different from the ways of thinking and looking of everyday life ; it implies a kind of divorce between science and society. Of course there is a distinction to be drawn between " pure " and " applied " science :

what else is the purpose of the two faculties in university structure, if not to emphasize the distinction ? But what I want to say is that the position and function of the " pure " scientist can be understood only if one studies the technological, economic, and ideological history which lies behind him, and the technological, economic, and ideological present into which he fits.

Now it is not my intention to attempt to trace the history of the sciences from those first practical fumblings with the planting of seeds, the making of fire, the smelting of metals, and the registration of astronomical regularities, down to the various technological discoveries which transformed man's views about the world and altered the balance of conflicting interests in societies through the ages, and on to the Industrial Revolution and its developments, marking along the route the emergence of specialists concentrating on particular kinds of problems. Such a task would be quite beyond me. My reason for turning your attention to the matter is that I want to suggest to you that the history and the nature of science are a part of social history, and that science starts with the practical problem of gaining a livelihood in the pursuit of which, as Malinowski has pointed out, the canons of scientific inference must be obeyed if success is to be achieved. The specialist, when he emerges, is the product of a certain climate of thought and belief; he is a member of a society with a certain socio-economic structure; he is confronted with problems characteristic of his age; what he does is determined in part by such circumstances, and in part by his own particular qualities. He may merely elaborate already existing techniques or theories; he may transform both. I do not for one moment wish to underestimate the significance of the scientific genius. On the contrary. Indeed I think some sociological theorists have gone too far in the direction of social determinism.

The individual genius is of supreme importance as a factor in social change. To suggest that a society discovered this, or that mankind discovered that, is ridiculous. Societies and mankind discover nothing, except in a very elliptical sense. Only individuals make discoveries. All I am saying is that the problems they tackle and the way they tackle them—the ideas and concepts they bring to bear—are conditioned (I do not say " determined ") by the social and economic structure within which they operate and by the religious, moral, and philosophical atmosphere in which they breathe. Furthermore, the changes they make in these structures and atmospheres are themselves conditioned by the state of affairs out of which they emerge.

So far I have been dealing with the natural sciences, and what I have said about social conditioning applies still more forcibly to psychology and sociology. If it is true that the natural sciences are, as it were, an elaboration of the day-to-day practical rules that everyone has to learn in order to cope with his physical environment, it is indeed the case that psychology and the social sciences are an elaboration of the day-to-day practical rules we have to apply in dealing with one another. It is true, of course, that while the non-specialists are applying such a general corpus of knowledge as has become common property the specialist in the natural sciences investigates new problems; and he makes discoveries which are surprising to his fellow men. And this is what makes it sound odd to say that his work is an " elaboration of day-to-day practical rules." I use the expression to link up the " pure " scientist with action. The surprises are due to the fact that the scientific discoverer in the field of the natural sciences is either handling old materials in a new way, or handling new materials altogether. He is enlarging the world in which we live and extending the scope of our action, much as the early explorers extended the world in which we live by discovering places previously unknown, and much as—in a microscopic region—the cook who discovers that the best way to cook brussels sprouts is to plunge them for five minutes into boiling water, is extending her culinary sphere and those of her friends to whom she reveals her secret.

Now with psychology and sociology all this seems to me to be different. If we say, very rightly, that psychology is the study of human behaviour, and sociology the study of social behaviour and its accompaniments, surely it is absurd to suggest that no one studied human beings and groups of human beings before Wundt and Comte. And I am not referring to the celebrities of the past whom I mentioned earlier. Surely man was studying woman from the very beginning in the Garden of Eden. And as to social psychology, it was applied with some effect by the serpent. Social science was applied in action by the first administrator. Man has been studying man, and men have administered their fellows, ever since men emerged and lived in groups large enough to call for the concept of " society." And this has gone on down the ages. No wonder the self-conscious and explicit study of men and society brings with it so few surprises. Even psycho-analysis is really an elaboration of what was already known : namely that certain people give bona fide reasons for doing things— reasons which other people know to be false. Let me hasten to say that I am not minimizing the importance of this. All I am saying is that psychology and sociology are quite obviously elaborations of ideas which we inevitably get from our everyday social intercourse with other people like ourselves. Unlike the fields of natural science, we are not coming across new materials, new places, new techniques—or very rarely; we are ever defining our concepts about the same old thing. It is this that depresses many modern psychologists. They want something new, something startling. And where do they look ? To physiology, of course. There they can find new physical materials, such as endocrine secretions, which influence human behaviour in unexpected ways. They study the physiology of conditioning and try to reduce it to a system. They handle the body in new ways, giving it electric shocks, pumping in insulin, or severing brain-fibres by pre-frontal leucotomy; and the results are startling indeed. But psychology, in the sense that we usually understand it—the study of men's behaviour in terms of conscious and unconscious motives—does not spring from the study of their nervous systems : it springs from the inevitabilities of social action, and so, I shall suggest, does sociology.

I have chosen social action as my topic because I think that social action is the basic concept in the social sciences. In this I am in agreement with Max Weber and his modern follower Talcott Parsons. The alternative claimants are : social relations, and societies-as-wholes. These concepts are, of course, useful, as I shall try to show, but they are not in my view fundamental. What do we mean by a social relationship ? Surely it is something derived from our observation of social action. Physical proximity is not a social relationship; it becomes so when we register by our conduct and its accompanying ideas that the person next door is a *neighbour*, to be treated with reserve or friendliness. Biological parenthood is not, as such, a social relationship; it becomes so when the mother and other people treat the infant as her legitimate or illegitimate child. A relationship is a social relationship in so far as it is established by social action.

The notion that a society-as-a-whole is the basic unit for social scientific study has even less to be said for it because it cannot be studied. The great Leviathan is not a whale: it is a construct—an "intervening variable," as some modern theorists would say. We cannot study societies as wholes any more than we can study personalities as wholes. What we mean when we say that we must study societies as wholes and personalities as wholes is that such organic concepts or integrated models are the most convenient tools for explaining social actions or individual conduct. Moreover, the very existence of a society-as-a-whole, or rather the registration of a particular aggregation of persons as a society-as-a-whole, depends on social action. Take a pair of compasses, draw a circle of any diameter you please upon a map, and it is doubtful whether you will happen to demarcate a society which should be treated as a whole. If you decide to make a social survey of a town, the first thing you have to decide is its boundaries. And you can do this only by inquiring into the social action of the authorities. Moreover, after the Local Government Act of 1929 the boundaries were changed here and there, so that what you might have taken as a society-as-a-whole in 1929 will be different in 1939, and much of what you said about the former will be inapplicable to the latter, though both have the same name.

So in the discussion of what the social scientist is studying and in the data whereby he verifies or falsifies his hypotheses we come back always to social action.

Let us now look more closely into the concept of social action. My first point is that all social action involves mutual adaptation. The conduct of A is determined by A's expectation of B's response, and B's response is determined by B's interpretation of A's conduct and the expectation he attributes to him, and also by his expectation of A's counter-response, and so on. This, as George Mead has pointed out, is true of the intercourse of animals below human level. The sexual, playful, and quarrelsome interaction of dogs and cats and birds all involve such mutual adaptation. So does the intercourse between humans and such domestic animals as interact with them. These range from such creatures as one can, as they say, " make pets of " to such creatures as one cannot because their interaction is limited to the mere approach to food and retreat from contact. With human beings the same " pet " level is found between the mother and her infant child. With human beings, however, something else is present. At some point in the evolutionary series creatures emerged whose gestures became not merely significant in the sense of eliciting appropriate responses, but significant to themselves—the point at which a gesture is awarefully directed to the eliciting of a response. How this came about we do not know. To say that the fore-brain became bigger does not help us until we know what goes on inside it. It may be that something like what George Mead suggested took place: that the turning point was the incipient adumbration in the actor of the response of the other, so that he, the actor, takes the role of the other in himself, thus paving the way for a contrast between his own " other " response, the *real* response of the other, and between both and his own spontaneous spring of activity. It may be that language, with its peculiar characteristics of being uttered and heard —both action and self-stimulus—by the actor, played a significant part in the development of man as such. We cannot go back and look. We can say that such feral men as have come to our notice—children brought up by animals or neglected by men—are scarcely human at all; but as for our own remote pre-human ancestry, we can but speculate. One thing seems to be plausible, and that is that only through social interaction at a level at which the awareful eliciting of counter-responses becomes possible do men become men, aware of themselves as separate beings having meaningful intercourse with one another.

And what happens then? I think one can get some insight into this by examining one or two trivial and very familiar experiences—so trivial that I feel somewhat apologetic about bringing them to your attention.

Imagine two friends who have been so related for some time. The actions of each when they are together are mutually adapted. After a while each can, as we say, " count upon " the other. In fact it is not merely that A can guess what B will do, as a psychiatrist can guess at the likely response of his patient, and it is not merely that B can guess what A will do, as, indeed, the patient may guess at the likely conduct of the psychiatrist. There is more to it than that. A knows that B knows what A is likely to do, and B knows what A expects B to expect. Something which one can call a mutually accepted system of expectations gets established. Each knows the other's little ways, and knows that the other knows his. There may, indeed, be unspoken secrets which each keeps from the other. Each has his own perspective in the duality; but for the relationship to persist there must be a mutual system controlling the conduct of both. The importance of this may indeed be realized when one reflects upon the common complaint you hear people make about some acquaintance: " Of course," they say, " you can't really make friends with him because he's so incalculable; you don't know what he's going to do next." Without a mutually accepted framework of behaviour no persistent social intercourse is possible. I would even extend this notion to hostility, though here there are complications. One enemy may destroy the other, and the relationship is at an end in default of one of the relata. The enemies may part and hate at a distance, and in some sense the relationship is at an end. They may, however, persist together or near at hand,

and then, as we all know, for the mutual hate to be kept up, a mutually accepted system of not speaking or passing nasty remarks, or reciprocal head-tossing must be preserved. That, surely, is one of the reasons why a soft answer turneth away wrath. That is why it takes two to make a quarrel.

Corresponding to the overt mutual adjustments and registering their consistency over a period we can conveniently endow the interacting parties with " frames of reference." This intervening variable we can build into that other construct: " personality," in terms of which we explain the total behaviour of each. By saying that persistent social intercourse engenders frames of reference I mean that each participant views and thinks of the other in terms of those expectations which he has acquired in the course of their friendship. Each will, as we say, " understand " the other, interpreting his gestures and his speech in terms of the mutual scheme which has become established.

And even this trivial example can be carried a little further. The two parties may, of course, interact to their mutual satisfaction without either of them mentioning the matter either to the other or to himself. On the other hand, they may, when perhaps the expectations of one are falsified: " I never expected you to do such a thing " one might say; then what I have called the scheme of accepted values may become symbolized as " our friendship." Doubtless the symbol will be slightly different in one from what it is in the other; but there must be common constituents, otherwise neither will be intelligible to the other. Again, it might be that one of them wants to do something which will cause pain to the other, something indeed which conflicts with their mutual system. Then he may say to himself: " I really ought not," or even, " I really *cannot* do this or that. It would ruin our friendship." Suppose, for instance, it is their wont to go to the pictures every Saturday night. Suppose A has an enticing invitation for one Saturday night. Will there not be a conflict in A's mind ? And, indeed, supposing both A and B receive an invitation for a Saturday night. Is it a gross exaggeration to suggest that they may say to one another: " Well, of course it means giving up *our* Saturday night's pictures " ? Something has been ever so slightly outraged. What, surely, has happened is that this day-to-day mutual scheme of inter-responses has become externalized and now stands out against them coercively. We are at once reminded of Durkheim's [1] definition of a social fact: " Un fait social se reconnait au pouvoir de coercition externe qu'il exerce ou est susceptible d'exercer sur les individus; et la présence de ce pouvoir se reconnait a son tour soit à l'existence de quelque sanction determinée, soit à la résistanse que le fait oppose à toute entreprise individuelle qui tend à lui faire violence." [2]

This going to the pictures on a Saturday night is, when we come to think of it, an institution of our society of two. It would be " wrong " of A to act in disaccord with its rules in despite of B, and even slightly " wrong " of A and B to alter it. And this, not only because of a cultural standard of " friendship,"—though of course any example I take will in fact bring this wider context in—but, I suggest, mainly because their relationship cannot continue without such mutually accepted norms. Certainly there are variations in the range of permissible behaviour when you compare two pairs of friends— as there are when you compare two societies on a larger

[1] *Règles de la Méthode Sociologique* (Presses Universitaires, 1947 edition), p. 11.
[2] A social fact may be recognized by the coercive pressure which it brings to bear on the individual from outside ; and the presence of this pressure can be detected either by the existence of some determinate sanction, or by the resistance which is set up against any attempt by the individual to violate the social fact.

scale—but some regulation there must be for any social relationship to persist.

What I am trying to suggest to you is that social institutions, law, and morality are the necessary products of all persistent social intercourse. Embryonically they are there even at the pre-human level, but their symbolization in language makes a vital difference. Without language I do not see how they could achieve the external validity they do achieve.

This becomes even clearer if we take a group larger than a pair. Imagine four people setting up house together: it might be four students. Again mutual adaptation of each to each, and each, in a sense, to all, is essential. They cannot, we will suppose, all sit on the same chair; they cannot all get into the bath at the same time. Problems arise, and a mutually acceptable solution must be found. The seating arrangements, the bath rota, the rules for washing up, and the times for meals will become established institutions; and any new-comer will find himself confronted with an order—let us say, " a culture "—not of his devising, external and coercive, to which he has to submit. The order will be felt to be " right "; that accommodation of conflicting interests, which we call " justice," will be achieved. I mentioned the new-comer, who is confronted with a pattern of interaction. How is it conveyed to him ? He might, of course, painstakingly watch and note the interlocking conduct, and form in his mind a patterned construct to represent it. More likely, of course, he will be told by the participants. " This," they might say, " is our way of life." It will have been symbolized.

And now increase this number. Let us suppose that the scheme is a success and that more students want to join. The group moves to larger quarters. They no longer, perhaps, consist of intimate friends, but acquaintances who have to be initiated. Mutual adjustment on a purely spontaneous basis becomes less reliable. The bath rota, the meal times, and so forth must be more strictly adhered to. Rules may even be written down on a sheet of paper and pinned up in the hall. Now let us suppose that in the early days each of our four friends took turns with the catering; there would not be much to do for four. But increased numbers, increased household expenses, increased responsibility for a larger establishment, present difficulties. One of their number might be specially good at dealing with them, perhaps the one who suggested the scheme in the first place—the leader or the eldest. Here the staging of my example in student circles becomes a little unrealistic, but I will ask you to bear with me, because the unrealism is really unimportant for my purpose. Let us suppose that this skilful organizer takes on the organizing as a whole-time job. To keep him contributions must be made, perhaps larger numbers still might be needed. The group incorporates anyone who wishes to join. A room is set aside for the organizer, now called the Warden. Note what has happened. The spontaneously interacting group of people who have precipitated their own norm in the course of living together has grown into an " enterprise "—a going concern. Organization brings with it its stratification; a hierarchy is in the offing. Administration has begun. A post, a social position with its appropriate role, has been created. *A new form of social action has come into being*. And look into the future. Generations of members have passed through the group. Wardens have come and gone, each judged not by his charm but by his efficiency. The group is enlarged still further, and along come an accountant, a secretary, a matron, and a staff of waiters. There are so many in the community that the Warden, who now sits upon a dais, cannot know them all. They are just anonymous students, mere names upon alphabetical lists, allotted rooms in order of application. The group has a name, a badge, a tie, and a yell. The picture of the founder hangs in a prominent place in the refectory. To go further would be frivolous. We might even imagine that when servants are in short supply, our establishment might capture the smaller hostel next door, incorporate it, and reduce its inhabitants to servitude.

Now I suggest that here we have, in an example not so fictitious as to be quite absurd, something very like what I think Hegel and Engels had in mind when they spoke of increase in quantity often leading to a change in quality. The impersonal world of administration produces frames of reference different from those which are developed in purely personal intercourse. They are explicitly symbolized and are applied to a different kind of content. The administrator's frame of reference, when he is playing his role, is not of such a kind as is brought into action when he thinks of: " My friendship with dear old George, who is so charming even when he does get het up, though of course he only does it in order to tease me." It is not like that at all. Whether he thinks in pictures or words or both, he thinks of a larger scheme with a name attached to it—the hostel, the business, the county, the city, the country, the party. He thinks in terms of individuals occupying certain positions in the concern which, as position, are relatively permanent. He thinks of the occupants as functionaries rather than as personalities, though of course he recognizes their personalities as making them good or bad role-players. And beside the functionaries, whom he might possibly name, there are the anonymous many who are administered for his own benefit, for the benefit of someone else, or for their own benefit. Here language is essential to the working of the scheme. Communications must run backward and forward, couched in terms which are intelligible to the intercommunicants. This means that the frame of reference of all involved, the key men and the masses, must have common elements. They too must think in terms of the hostel, the business, the county, the city, the country, the party, or whatever type of concern they, as we say, belong to. In fact I would say that "belonging," in anything more than a purely classificatory sense, positively *means* thinking in such terms.

But thinking in terms of the concern is by no means the whole story. In the first place, each member will see it from his own point of view; but their points of view must contain common elements for communication to be possible. The student thinks of himself as a student at Birmingham University, the lecturer as a lecturer at Birmingham University, the lab-steward as lab-steward at Birmingham University, and so on. They all mean something the same by "Birmingham University." Secondly, each will have an attitude towards the concern. He may identify himself with it and act with enthusiasm in terms of its regulations and in terms of his notion of the accepted ethos; he may dissociate himself from the concern, merely keeping the rules in order to avoid the consequences of breaking them; or he may be indifferent to the concern but keep the rules because life is simpler that way; or break them when he thinks he can get away with it. But whichever he does, he must have somewhat the same notion of the concern and its rules as his fellow members. The future history of the concern will of course in part depend on the proportions of those who identify themselves with it as compared with those who dissociate themselves from it, and the intensity of their feelings, which, in turn, will be largely dependent on their conscious or unconscious interests.

Now all the time we must remember that within the concern, whatever it may be, there is always personal intercourse going on, with its mutual adjustments, its private codes of behaviour, its crises, and their resolutions. The administrator has his wife, his daughter, his cronies, and his carpet slippers. Indeed, one of the administrated, meeting him *en pantouffles*, may say afterwards : " the old man was really quite human "—a significant phrase. And yet, again, these private affairs occur upon a public stage. Thus we must fuse or combine our frames of reference. Every man is both a " private person " and a " public personage "—using the latter phrase in no status-conferring sense. He is in love with, devoted to, or indifferent to, the woman with whom he shares his leisure hours; at the same time he is her husband, her fiancé, or her lover. One evening he is with his intimates, but has to leave them to take the chair at a meeting. He is having dinner with his friend Tom and is called away to a patient.

And so we might go on, but we must beware of imputing the analytical world view of the social scientist to the subjects of his study without qualification. A man's conduct is less awarefully governed than we are apt to imagine. It is ridiculous to suppose that a person says to himself: " Now I am a private person, now I am a civil servant, foreign secretary, dustman," or whatever position he may occupy. The analytic view is seen through the frame of reference of the sociologist. Nevertheless we can say that every man and woman is brought up to develop a kind of double world in which he or she lives: a world of immediacies set in a context of remoter relationships, institutions, beliefs, and concerns. We all live as it were in L'Hôtel de l'Univers et de Portugal. A man works beside Fred, a decent sort of chap even if he is a bit of a boozer; his face-to-face intercourse with Fred takes place in a context of the firm who employs them, and that is situated in a city, and the city in a country which has relations with other countries in the world. Sometimes the man thinks in terms of Fred's

Freddishness, if I may be allowed the expression, sometimes in terms of " the firm," and sometimes in terms of " the country." He has learnt to handle Fred partly by past experience with other people, and partly by trial and error with Fred himself; he has learnt to think in terms of the firm and the country because these concepts have been conveyed to him in language. In the latter case there is no direct contact because in some sense the firm and the country exist only in virtue of the agreed conventions of the people he meets and of multitudes of other people whom he does not meet. Of course there has to be a material substratum for it all; there have to be other human beings able to do things with their hands and with machines; there have to be materials to mould into the desired shapes; there have to be buildings in which this is done. Without all this the notion of " the firm " will not come into existence. All the same, the accumulation of these articles in one place is the result of social action. Our worker does not merely mean by " the firm " these physical things: he means the whole concern with its positions of manager and foreman, its profit-making, its clocking-in system, and so on, within which the men, machine, and building have their meaning.

Now not all of the world-views I have been discussing are of equal importance to the sociologist. There are some which more closely approximate to the one he is trying to formulate. The world of the peasant may be limited by the boundaries of his village with a vague penumbra behind his religion and the fruits of his labour, a vague notion of distant co-believers and tax-collectors. He is more concerned with day-to-day personal contacts. The administrator, as we have seen, has a different and wider view. He thinks in terms of countries, of cities, of economic problems. He, indeed, has the sociological view. The sociologist, I suggest, is the specialist who tries to elaborate and make precise the administrative world-picture.

I have put the whole matter in this way because I want to make two points. In the first place, just as the first man who moulded metal was the first metallurgist, so the first person who awarefully considered the character of the person he was dealing with was the first psychologist; and the first administrator, whether chief or warrior, who thought in terms of the tribe, the clan, or the army, was the first sociologist. Metallurgy, psychology, and sociology as scientific disciplines arise when thought about these things becomes too complicated for the practical man. In the second place, the emergence of psychology and sociology is a natural development from the necessities of social action when performed by creatures capable of reflection and symbolic registration.

We cannot penetrate the night of time. We can, I think, plausibly assume that something like this happened. In the beginning was the word. Our ancestors at some point or other began to use words meaningfully and not as mere emotive utterances. They were then capable of symbolizing the rules according to which their social action was conducted, and handed on these rules to their children. Then, when technology enabled large numbers to keep together, a more complicated régime was necessary to ensure their efficient co-operation, and this means social action at the administrative level, with the appropriate conceptual superstructure. Once this is established and gets verbalized, then the ball is set rolling from those distant ages down to our own times. The whole apparatus of sociological analysis is there from the start: law, morality, beliefs, society, technology, economics, politics, the in-group, the out-group, the face-to-face group, the indirectly-related group, the system of positions and accompanying roles, and moreover, even the embryonic concept of status, whereby some are accepted as higher than others.

It will, I dare say, be objected that I have concentrated too much on human beings interacting with one another and that I have left their material cond:tions out of account. This is only because one cannot say everything at once. Of course the development of societies depends on material conditions, the appraisal of them as valuable or indifferent, and the presence or absence of things to appraise. And each generation is brought up to apprehend the significance of the physical environment as understood by the technological standards of its parents. Their own efforts will change the world both materially and evaluatively for their progeny, often in ways which they did not expect, and the stage is set for another act.

In stressing the vital importance of men's *ideas* of the groups to which they belong, I may be accused of treating the whole subject too mentalistically; I may be accused of idealism, in some of the many senses of that term of abuse. But surely mental talk is the only talk we can use. Picture a little boy in a forest; along the path comes a man; the lad peeps out to see who is coming so that he can prepare himself for appropriate behaviour. It might be his maternal uncle, it might be a relation with whom it is incumbent upon him to joke or tell dirty stories, it might be the chief. The boy will recognize the on-comer and act accordingly. " He knows who it is, he has learnt how to behave, he believes that certain conduct is right and certain conduct is wrong," we say. And will any physiological story about the intruder be more helpful? X-ray him, subject him to electro-encephalography, dissect him, tell us all you can about his physical make-up, and now tell us whether he really was the boy's maternal uncle or not. And the boy himself? Look into his fore-brain for traces and you will have to interpret your findings in terms of the boy's actual conduct. It may, of course, well be that in the future we shall be able to peer into the nervous system of such a little boy and say, *before* he acts: " See, that neural explosion is the maternal-uncle index; now he will be neurally caused to do so and so." But such predictive powers lie in the future. We can make our little curtsy to some useless but fashionable form of materialism and say what is doubtless true: " It all depends on our brains." Then we must pass on to talk in terms which are intelligible.

Again I may be accused of psychologism—of saying that we can understand and interpret social events by direct reference to human intentions. I am saying no such thing. Human intentions are certainly basic to social happenings, but the social happenings themselves are frequently—more often than not—unintended. Each of our two friends had intentions, but they did not intend to precipitate the coercive social fact of friendship. We intend to reap where we have sown, but we did not intend to make a dust-bowl. Men and women intend to have fewer children, they do not intend to alter the age-structure of the population. Once an agreed structure is established with its appropriate frames-of-reference, as a resultant of the interaction of individuals, whether the structure be tribalism, the slave state, feudalism, capitalism, or communism, individuals privately intend to do this or that within whatever context they may be operating. The result of the totality of their private intentions—desires for money, prestige, sexual intercourse, or the satisfaction of curiosity—will be the perpetuation, the alteration, the transformation, or the destruction of the social pattern. But the result cannot be attributed to the individual wishes of any one of them, save perhaps to a very few in key positions.

I have suggested, then, that social action takes place between persons who agree among themselves that they hold certain positions in a social structure. As participants in that structure they have been brought up to entertain certain beliefs. And they and their fellow participants are confronted by certain physical opportunities and hazards, including among them the number of participants there are.

Thus we have four aspects of social action to study: interaction itself; the social constructs within which it is performed; the beliefs which it produces and which in turn guide it; and the physical and demographic environment in which it takes place. These four aspects I hope to disentangle in the next chapter.

CHAPTER II

Personality, Society, and Culture

EARLIER I have suggested that two forms of social interaction can be distinguished: face-to-face mutual adaptation, and indirect administrative decision-making. The second springs out of, but does not of course displace, the first; it comes about when numbers make direct face-to-face contact impossible for all members of the interacting group at once—when, that is to say, something like a chain system of interaction is required. Out of the many prerequisites of social action on these two levels come four interlocking fields of study: face-to-face interaction itself; the social structure in which it occurs; the system of beliefs (in the widest sense of this word) which it precipitates and in terms of which it is carried on; and the physical and demographic environment which conditions it and which is in turn altered by it.

Now one of the difficulties of exposition lies in the fact that one cannot divide one's voice into four voices, each speaking at once about one of these four aspects of social life. Everything would be much easier if some musical form could be constructed in which, perhaps, the sopranos could speak of beliefs, as in Handel's *Messiah*: "I know that my Redeemer liveth" —which is apposite enough in some quarters these days; the contraltos might discourse on the contemporary role-system; the tenors on private life; while the basses would rumble away about the background of supply and demand. This, however, is impossible; but the idea is not as frivolous as it sounds, for we always have to remember that interaction on the personal level, which in some important sense is all that there *is*, takes place within a mutually understood social system, characterized by its own system of beliefs and conditioned by the material and personal resources at the command of its members.

Every infant born today is born into an on-going concern, into a " social system." In the somewhat repellent language of Talcott Parsons, " a social system consists in a plurality of individual actors interacting with each other in a situation which has at least a physical or environmental aspect, actors who are motivated in terms of a tendency to the ' optimization of gratifica-tion ' and whose relation to their situation, including each other, is defined and mediated in terms of a system of culturally structured and shared symbols." [1] His personality will be conditioned partly by his own poten-tialities and partly by the cultural norms prevailing in the social system of which he is brought up to be a member. The persistence of norms as such is due to the pre-requisites of social action on a large scale, and they are verbalized and handed down from generation to genera-tion. The particular norms prevailing are the resultant of the various historical changes which have occurred in the past, among which the most significant are changes in the techniques of satisfying material needs and desires together with the shifts of inter-personal relationships which accompany them.

One obvious topic of study is the reactions of indivi-dual organisms to the demands made of them by the normative regulations of the social system into which they are born, as mediated by the adults and coevals with whom they come into contact, who will act towards it in terms of their own version of appropriate behaviour. Such investigations will lead to the formulation of

[1] *The Social System* (Tavistock Publications, 1952), p. 5.

theories to account for the way in which the organic reactions are systematized into the construct which we call "personality," in terms of which we attempt to understand and predict conduct. This is a vast field of study, and this is not the appropriate place to discuss the various theories which have been put forward.

I may, however, call attention to a certain change which can be detected when we compare recent personality psychology with the personality psychology of the past. Cross-cultural research, associated for example with the name of one of my predecessors in this series of Josiah Mason lectures, Dr Margaret Mead, has so enlarged our perspective that any theory about the development of personality has to be applicable to a wide variety of cultural contexts. The Freudian theory is applicable, in so far as it is applicable at all, to a patrilineal culture with relatively small household units and a long and close dependence of children on the care and approbation of only one or two persons. It is not applicable to many matrilineal societies, nor to societies where a child is attended to by a large number of adults indifferently. Horney and Fromm, the so-called neo-psychoanalysts, have attempted to formulate more general principles applicable to a wider range of cultural pressures. The main emphasis in such studies has been on what may be called the pathological aspect of development. Broadly speaking, granted adequate potentialities, children can be brought up to exhibit and admire a very wide range of personality traits: those of warriors, capitalists, industrious peasants, or servants of the community, provided there is sufficient reward to compensate for the deprivations incident upon training. When, however, the rewards are inadequate—and it might be that no reward is adequate to compensate for, say, extreme deprivation of sexual desire—or where from case to case in any society inadequate recognition of social worth has been forthcoming, or where, as among the Alorese, inadequate security is a characteristic of the general cultural method of child-rearing—in such cases typical reactions ensue.

It is, I think, generally agreed that among the needs which a culture has to satisfy we must include something which may be called the need of a sense of social worth. We do not have to fall back upon any bogus " explanation " in terms of a gregarious instinct to account for this. It is a need acquired through the long dependence of human offspring on the care of adults.   They have learnt, as their parents and ancestors have learnt before them, that only through other people can their needs be met, and then only if they are " good " and fit in the approved fashion into the wide social system which surrounds them. If they get that approval and assurance, all may be well.   If they do not, then they must defend themselves against their deepening sense of insecurity.   They may rebel, so as to persuade themselves that they are secure enough to do so; they may withdraw into their shells so as to avoid contact with a potentially hostile world; or they may passionately seek the companionship of others with whom they can feel safe.   The significance of this for the understanding of deviant conduct will be referred to again later.

The study of the development and moulding of personalities through social interaction is only one of the topics which the general field of social interaction at the face-to-face level includes.   We have the indefinitely large range of human intercourse before us.   Some types of interaction will be mentioned farther on and some methods of analysis of interaction in small groups will be described in Chapter Four.

But let us now turn to the concept of the social system within which these interactions take place.   And, in passing, I would remind you that the social system of which I write is an abstraction constructed from the concrete interactions which are our only evidence.

I think the most helpful conceptual tools with which to construct social systems are those forged by Linton and Talcott Parsons. The latter is the more complicated of the two, and though I shall draw heavily upon his work, I can make no attempt to guide you through the vast tangled labyrinth of his writings. Both these authors analyse a social system into a network of positions and their accompanying roles. There are certain positions which any individual may occupy because of his or her biological qualifications: such are the positions of infant, boy, girl, adolescent, adult male, adult female, husband, wife, father, mother, maternal uncle, cross-cousin, old man, or old woman. Such positions will have a range of appropriate conduct attached to them, and these are the appropriate roles. Positions like these Linton calls " ascribed." There are, however, in most societies, positions the filling of which depends on certain personal qualifications and skills: such are the positions of priest, medicine man, lawyer, member of parliament, baker, and professional thief. These positions, again, have appropriate conduct attached to them, and such positions Linton calls " achieved." With these simple notions any social system can be described in terms of the positions which make it up and the socially accepted roles which the occupants are expected to play. At the same time it is important not to over-simplify our picture. We must distinguish between the conventional expectation, the notion of which certainly guides the individual when he is playing his part, and the role-playing itself, which is performed in a style partly determined by the unique characteristics of the player.

This highly abstract scheme has been elaborated by Parsons, who groups roles according to five criteria. (1) There are roles in which the player may seek immediate gratification in the actual social action in which he is engaged; on the other hand, there are roles in which immediate gratification is a secondary consideration, even if considered at all, roles in which the actor is carrying out his act in pursuit of a remoter end. The confusion of these types of role is illustrated by the young lady at the post office selling stamps to her boy friend. She should have more of what Parsons calls " affective neutrality." (2) There are roles, such as that of the capitalist entrepreneur, in which the actor may properly seek his own ends; on the other hand, there are roles, such as those of doctor or judge, where the actor's conduct should be collectively orientated. Examples of confusion of these roles may easily be imagined. (3) In some positions the occupier is expected to conduct himself in terms of the general category to which the others, towards whom his role is directed, belong. A doctor should treat all his patients with equal care, so must a lawyer his clients; the man at the labour exchange must treat all applicants with equal consideration. There must, indeed, be no favouritism. In other positions this is not the case. A son is expected to behave in a special way towards his parents because of their particular relation to him. The charge of " nepotism " is heard when a man in what Parsons calls a " universal " position plays a " particularistic " role. (4) The three preceding distinctions are concerned with the actor and the various standards by which he should play his various roles. The fourth distinction is rather concerned with alternative attitudes towards the actor as a social object. Do we judge him by his performance, by his efficiency; or do we judge him by his qualities, by what he *is* ? In some social situations we focus our attention on his achievement; in others we focus attention on his personal qualities, as for example in the case of a charismatic leader or dictator, who may have won his position by achievement or by birth, but whose specific qualities are what we react to and have expectations about.

(5) Finally, our intercourse sometimes demands of us a diffuse range of duties, as in the case of the mother who is expected to care for her child in all manner of ways; while in other situations the actor is expected mainly to provide a single service, as in the case of the shop-assistant.

This analysis is deduced from certain primary assumptions about the nature of social action, and space will not permit me to give any account of the argument. The interest lies in the claim that these five pairs of alternative standards are (a) necessitated by the nature of social intercourse, (b) are an exhaustive list of possible alternatives. This means that all social systems can be analysed into networks of positions and their roles, every one of which is characterized by some combination or other of these five pairs. Whether this claim can be made good or not can be decided only after a considerable amount of research; but even if the list is not exhaustive it has an interim value for descriptive purposes. It is clear, I think, that we can distinguish social systems from one another by noting the salient combinations which, as it were, set the tone of the society. A kinship system is mainly composed of positions in which the occupant behaves to other people mainly in terms of their *particular* relationship to him; his own position is *ascribed* to him by his relation to them, a general diffuseness of duties is required of him, and he may be expected to seek his enjoyment in the actual carrying out of such duties. In our own western capitalism the positions are mainly such as to demand affective neutrality, self-seeking, and achievement in specific jobs in which the particular relationships of the actors and those towards whom they act are irrelevant. In the People's Republic of China, so far as one can gather from a brief visit, collectivity-orientation is dominant; people are expected to get immediate enjoyment out of the work they are doing; the categories of persons dealt with are treated without favouritism; positions are ascribed to those fitted by ability and education to fill them.

A problem to be raised on page 83 crops up here with the first pair of alternatives. Everyone demands emotional satisfaction, enjoyment in the here-and-now situation. In a kinship system this may be provided for by the particular and personal intercourse which such interaction provides. In a society with the emphasis laid upon collective orientation, enjoyment may be provided by high social rewards being given for services, with the addition, perhaps, of the accessible goodwill of a charismatic and loving leader, whose image is seen upon every wall and can be worn in any buttonhole, and for whose personal approval any sacrifice is worth while. In the affective neutral achievement-orientated half of the world in which we live, present emotional satisfaction is liable to be a hindrance to getting on, which is the dominant theme. This emotional starvation is, I think, rightly regarded as one of the most potent factors in causing the *malaise* of the western world.

A social system, then, is a system of positions and roles, each of which has certain standards of performance and attitude attached to it. This analysis, however, is clearly far too abstract for the delineation of any particular system. To get an adequate construct we have to organize the participants who occupy the positions offered according to other criteria, because these further considerations lend meaning to the positions themselves and the roles which are associated with them. There are at least five modes of organization which must be conceived of as mutually conditioning, each the others, in terms of that *consensus* which Comte believed to be the key to social statics. These five aspects of social structure are the kinship system, the economic system, the political system, what I will call the cellular system, and the status system.

It is obvious that in order to get an adequate description and explanatory model we require to know the details of all these five. Is the destiny of the individual determined by his position in an elaborate matrilineal or patrilineal network of kin; or are his kinship affiliations reduced within a small compass ? Do the actors in the social system satisfy their needs and desires by hunting and food-gathering, or by elementary gardening, or by the keeping of flocks and herds, or by extensive agricultural activities which produce a sufficient surplus to provide for armies and city-dwellers as well as for primary producers ? Have they reached a stage of technical proficiency which enables them to develop industry and trade together with the ancillary devices of banking and the formation of joint enterprises ? Have they reached that stage of vast concerns when ownership and control are in different hands, and where the technician and the manager are of more consequence than those who benefit from the profits ? The classification of societies according to their political structure is even more obvious and has occupied the attention of writers in the western world from the days of Aristotle down to our own, and it would be superfluous for me to weary you with a list of the possible variations.

The kinship, economic, and political régimes are not all that we want to know. In all but the simplest societies, social systems contain within them sub-systems which cannot conveniently be listed under these three headings, though they are largely conditioned by them. I call this, for want of a better phrase, the " cellular structure " of the society, and by it I mean those groupings of people into associations such as secret societies, religious sects, professional bodies, learned societies, trade unions, pig clubs, and so forth; and into geographical groupings of habitation such as villages, market towns, and cities. This cellular structure, as I have called it, is concerned not only with the bare facts of sub-groups and their membership, whether on a mutual interest basis or on the basis of geographical proximity; it is also concerned with the question of whether the actors in the social systems participate in associational groupings at the expense, perhaps, of what is called " community life." It has been suggested with some plausibility that men and women living in large cities pursue their various interests by joining with others who share them, which means joining different associations according to the different interests for which they cater. They go their various ways, and that mutual interest in local affairs and local persons which constitutes a community and a neighbourhood unit does not develop. This again brings us back to the problem of the satisfaction of man's need for a sense of social security which has been mentioned before, and the question as to what forms of social participation provide him with what he needs.

Finally we come to social stratification. The inclusion of this in our model of any social system is obvious enough, but its mention enables me to make a point of some importance. The kinship system of a primitive tribe is a relatively clear-cut formal affair which all the members recognize, even if some of them do not know the details. The economic and political organizations, too, can be described in terms acceptable to all participants, even though, again, many of them may not be fully aware of the whole story. But even in the formal kinship system there may be disputes about ancestry: conflicting evidence may come before the inquiring anthropologist, and my predecessor, Professor Raymond Firth,[1] has shown how various permitted devices ease the working out of strict formal obligations when conflicts and problems arise. He bids us make our formal

[1] *Elements of Social Organization* (Watts, 1951).

structure more flexible by the inclusion of the concept of social organization. Similarly with the political structure: we can identify the position and mark out the spheres of formal competence, but what actually happens is in part due to the personal qualities and acquired traditions of the role-players. The civil servant's duty is, no doubt, to carry out the policy of his Minister; but it is also his duty to give advice, and we should get a distorted and unrealistic picture if we ignored the powers of a consolidated body of knowledgeable men confronted by a Minister less well equipped than they are. Similarly, in the world of economic activity we may have constructed a stereotype of the entrepreneur, which by no means adequately represents the variety of policies which govern the decisions of the occupants of this position at any time. The difficulty is that our formal structure must be complicated by introducing informal actualities, if our framework is to be of any use. Indeed, I would say that one of the jobs of the sociologist is to make our models more flexible and more complicated by the investigation of what actually happens.

All this is peculiarly the case with social stratification. We may start with a clear-cut pattern of castes in India, but we soon learn that pretensions to hierarchical positions *vis-à-vis* the Brahmin caste vary from one part of India to another, and that various conventions have to be adopted to cope with the increased chances of pollution introduced by modern transport. The formal stereotype of western feudalism is a gross misrepresentation of that restless age of shifting loyalties and alternatives of insecure domination. When we come to our own age the vagueness of our social stratification is even more obvious. In a recent inquiry,[1] in which a technique rather like that used by Robert Centers in America was

[1] *Some Psychological Aspects of Social Structure*, by F. M. Martin (MSc Thesis, Univ. of London).

employed, some 400 men and women living in Greenwich and 400 living in Hertford were classified according to occupation—itself a far more difficult proceeding than we might imagine. The occupations were arranged in a hierarchy of prestige which had been worked out by a research team at the London School of Economics. The 800 subjects were asked : How many social classes are there ?   To which do you belong ?   Who else belongs to the same class ?   And who belongs to the other ones ? I am not quoting the actual questions.   Broadly speaking, the people in managerial capacity and the professions called themselves " middle class " and were so called by all the others.   Some of the salaried non-manual workers called themselves " middle class " and some " working class," while the manual workers divided themselves in a similar way.   A significant proportion of the salaried workers who claimed working-class status had fathers who were manual workers, while the manual workers who claimed middle-class status thought of the working class as idle ne'er-do-wells.   All groups showed different notions of class alignment; that is to say, the class-structure aspect of the general picture of the society in which they lived varied from one perspective to another. This is, of course, not startling news, but it means that when we speak of *the* class structure of a society, we must ascertain whether we are constructing a scheme which is the same as that agreed on by all the members, or whether we should construct a composite scheme of varying perspectives with only a few points of mutual agreement.

But supposing we construct our system with its kinship, economic, political, cellular, and class aspects which give significance to the positions of which it is composed, this will provide us only with a static framework, the description of a frozen society.   We must look to the dynamic aspect; our model must be a live one. If we look round at the five aspects of which we have taken account and ask ourselves in which sphere should we look for the key to the *consensus* of them all, we cannot for a moment deny the Marxist claim that it is the sphere of economics. Much in any given social system may derive from culture contact; much, particularly among primitive peoples, may have to be attributed to unique inventions in peculiar circumstances; and much may be due to the autonomous development of belief systems operating according to their own rules of consistency. This is true, but such factors cannot displace the economic structure from its dominant position. With very simple technological means at their disposal an enormous variety of alternative patterns may be woven, but certain patterns are impossible. As technological equipment advances and individual men can become rich, a kinship system is threatened and is bound either to collapse or to attempt to class commerce as a degraded occupation as in ancient Japan, or to control it with ill effects on its efficiency as in ancient China, the ill effects being in part due to the intrusion of particularist values in a universalistic context.

But the primacy of economic change as a determinant of general social change is more apparent when one considers its effect on political and status structure, and on those cellular groupings which have an economic foundation. In *Oceana*, written in 1656, James Harrington insisted that (I quote R. H. Tawney) [1]: " Different property systems have different types of government as their necessary consequence. Great demesnes in the hands of a prince become the foundation of an absolute monarchy; mixed monarchy arises when the estates of the nobility overshadow those of the rest of the nation and enable them to deal on equal terms with the ruler;

[1] " Harrington's Interpretation of His Age " (Raleigh Lecture on History, 1941), *Proc. Brit. Acad.*, Vol. XXVII.

a wide distribution of land among the masses of the population produces the popular sovereignty properly known by the term ' Commonwealth.' " But, " when the crown sheds its estates but continues to claim the power which formerly it owed to them; or when the nobility is bought out by a rising middle class but will not abdicate its privileges; or when the unprivileged masses lose their hold on the land but cling nevertheless to rights which they can no longer enforce, the result, whether tyranny, as in the first case, or oligarchy, as in the second, or anarchy as in the third, is an interlude of dislocation." Such, too, was the view of Machiavelli, and other writers of that age. In our own age such a method of analysis, carried out with greater subtlety and better information than was at the disposal of James Harrington, is the outstanding contribution of Marxist writers to sociology. Unless one incorporates the dynamic clash of interests in the economic field into one's social structure, the picture one constructs is useless. In no other field do changes have so profound an effect. Comte's *consensus* is dominated by technology and the relations of production in the sense that when changes occur in these to the development of which the existing social structure is maladjusted, then a mounting tension is set up which must lead to a new adjustment. At the same time it must be noted, as Max Weber has pointed out in his studies of Indian and Chinese religious systems, economic changes themselves can take place only in certain social structures. The economic field is no more autonomous than any other field of human activity. An economic system, with its appropriate political organization, may be so firmly established and held in position by the power of those who reap the benefits, backed by a deep respect for tradition, that no economic changes of any magnitude can take place at all. Other factors of significance are the type of military organization in any period and changes in the methods of warfare due to the development of new techniques of fighting.

Finally, we may add to our descriptive model the concept of *function*. Round this notion controversy rages, a controversy into which I do not propose to enter, though something will have to be said about the issues in the next chapter. At this juncture we may take the concept of function in its most obvious meaning. A social system is an on-going concern, with its positions organized in kinship, economic, political, cellular, and hierarchical formations. We can speak of the functions of certain positions with respect to the way in which the roles associated with them lead to ends deemed by all or by some members of the society to be desirable. Thus we can speak of the function of the lawyer, the doctor, the accountant, or the priest. Again, we can speak of those approved systems of social action, which we call institutions, as having a function; we speak of the function of primary education, of banking, of the civil service, and so forth. This is obvious enough, but it is by no means all. Such functions as I have mentioned are what R. K. Merton calls " manifest functions " in the sense that we are referring to " objective consequences contributing to the adjustment of adaptation of the system which are intended and recognized by partici-pants in the system." [1]

Now, I have already mentioned that the sociologist is interested in the unintended results of human intentions. The student of economics is to a large extent concerned with such matters. Put at its simplest, if certain goods are in short supply the consumption of some of them may intensify the demand and the price may rise. The consumer wants to satisfy his needs or desires; he does not intend to cause a rise in prices. This elementary example could obviously be multiplied indefinitely.

[1] *Social Theory and Social Structure* (Free Press, 1951), p. 51.

Again, the Nonconformist preachers of the nineteenth century intended to save the souls of those to whom they ministered; they did not intend to divert the attention of the poor from their exploitation. The Welfare State is intended to provide for minimum needs, it is not intended as a device to stave off revolution. And yet these unintended results may *de facto* be the case. Merton calls the production of these factual and unintended consequences " the latent functions " of whatever produces them, and he goes so far as to say that the " distinctive intellectual contributions of the sociologist are found primarily in the study of unintended consequences (among which are latent functions) of a given practice as well as in the study of anticipated consequences (among which are manifest functions)." [1]

Now I must leave this topic of social structure, and turn to the current system of belief and taste. Social actions are performed in an environment rendered meaningful by empirical and non-empirical belief systems, and saturated with evaluation. They are performed in terms of an accepted value system, and they are related to that mixture of empirical belief and standards of value for which Parsons uses the somewhat uncomfortable word " ideology." This he defines as follows: " An ideology is a system of beliefs, held in common by the members of a collectivity, i.e. a society, or a sub-collectivity of one—including a movement deviant from the main culture of the society—a system of ideas, which is oriented to the evaluative integration of the collectivity, by interpretation of the empirical nature of the collectivity and of the situation in which it is placed, the processes by which it has developed to its given state, the goals to which its members are collectively oriented, and their relation to the future course of events." [2]

[1] op. cit. p. 53.   [2] op. cit. p. 349.

Systems of empirical belief spring from man's awareful manipulation of the physical world and of his fellows. Systems of morality, principles of justice, and the regulative principles of criminal law spring from the prerequisites of social action at the personal and administrative levels. The derivative of non-empirical beliefs is not, I must confess, so clear. The material of which they are constructed can doubtless be derived from the personification of natural forces, the animation of fortuitous helps and hindrances in everyday life, speculations about man's destiny, and the projection into a heavenly world of his schemes of government and his domestic psychological predicaments. All these hypotheses have been put forward, and doubtless others as well, but, as Durkheim has pointed out, they none of them account for the distinction between the " sacred " and the " profane," which supplies the differentiating characteristic of religion. Durkheim himself, of course, explained the " sacred " in terms of the apprehension by the individual of the pull of society upon him, but there are serious difficulties in this account. The social pull does not always present itself in this form. There is much to be said for the view that a function of religion is to add supernatural sanction to morality. There is much to be said for Malinowski's view that one of its functions may be to consolidate the group in time of affliction and to surround important features of group life with an aura of dignity and solemnity. There is much also to be said for the view that religious beliefs may from time to time be used as an opiate, dulling the senses of the oppressed.

But all these views presuppose some core, some attitude, some emotional response which lies at the basis of religion, whatever may be the elaboration of its content. The believers, of course, have a ready answer to the problem : there is a divine world, and religions are man's misapprehension of it.   To the non-believer such a solution is unpalatable, and I have to confess that I can find no satisfactory explanation.   The currently accepted explanations seem to me to imply the existence of that which they are trying to explain, or, as in the case of Durkheim's more profound study, are unsatisfactory for other reasons. We must just accept and give due weight to religious systems as we find them.

They, together with the rest of the material which make up the sphere of human beliefs, values, and tastes, provide, of course, an inexhaustible field of inquiry for the curious.   Later on I propose to deal with the problem of the social influences which condition the belief systems from one age to another.   At the moment I only want to make one point.   I have already said that these systems of beliefs, values, and tastes, which we have to consider separately, because it is impossible to say everything at once, must be taken as constitutive of the real world in which actors act, though we must remember that in a large-scale society the " culture-world," if I may invent the expression for the moment—using the word " culture " in the popular sense—will vary from one section of it to another.   The working man in our society knows but a fraction of science, a fraction ever growing larger, and his value system—as I shall presently suggest— may well be different from that of the middle classes; his tastes, too, are different.   There are sects and cliques, learned societies and spiritualist groups, all with their different culture-worlds, each as real to its denizens as another is real to their neighbours.   But in addition to this, beliefs, values, and tastes may also be not matters of acceptance, but matters for contemplation without acceptance.   We can consider and discuss beliefs without believing.   Furthermore, there are what we might call belief, value, and taste specialists, concerned with general problems of science, of morality, and of æsthetics.

4

The pure scientific specialist—and I do not mean " specialist " in the narrow sense—is interested in scientific research for its own sake; the moral philosopher is interested in moral problems as such; and the æsthetician is interested in the criticism and production of works of art. I have not, of course, mentioned all the cultural specialists; but the ones I have mentioned will serve my purpose, and I want to include among them people who at first sight might not seem to belong. I want to include among the moral philosophers, the moral teachers—such as Confucius, Buddha, Jesus Christ, and Marx—and I want to include among the æstheticians, artists of all kinds. The point I wish to make is that practitioners in these cultural spheres have a certain autonomy of their own. The pure scientist, when he emerges, carries on his investigation in accordance with the rules of scientific inference to a certain extent independent of the social structure in which he functions. Problems are set for him by the social needs of his age; he has to start with the scientific views of his time; but no knowledge of these will enable us to infer the advances he may make.

The central core of morality is justice. The command to take cognizance of the other is inherent, as I have suggested, in social intercourse as such. Development in moral ideas, as Ginsberg [1] has pointed out, is a process of enlarging the range over which considerations of justice are significant, and weeding out those irrelevant considerations which have given rise to over- or under-estimation of claims. The general social preconditions of this are, I agree, the enlargement of the sphere of social contacts and the increased economic power of those whose claims have been overridden. All the same, I think that the moral contemplative, the moral teacher, plays his part in furthering what I would be prepared to

[1] *Reason and Unreason in Society* (LSE, 1947), pp. 307 f.

call moral logic, and in giving expression to wider moral outlooks.

The artist in all fields is doubtless conditioned by the social structure in which he writes, or paints, or composes. And yet, from a knowledge that he must paint portraits for the rich, one cannot infer the style in which he will paint them—a style which in turn may influence his successors, either making them do something of the same kind, or making them do something explicitly different.

My point is that in an age in reaction against an overestimation of the powers and status of ideas, we must be careful not to falsify the picture in the other direction by saying that which logically deprives them of all influence whatever.

I have left to the last the fourth topic—the material environment, including under that expression what is conveyed by human statistics. I have left it to the last because I propose to say something about human statistics in the next chapter, and because the influence and importance of the geographical environment are so very obvious. Geographical conditions, in which I include climate and the natural flora and fauna, present opportunities and set initial limits. The degree to which they condition human social life is contingent upon the way in which humans can exploit what they have to offer. The School of Le Play may have overestimated geographical influence, but they talked a great deal of sense. Indeed, when one is dealing with primitive societies one cannot understand their structure unless one knows the way in which they have exploited their geographical environment. The Comanche Indian, when he lived a difficult life on the plateau, valued the old men as repositories of wisdom; they descended to the plains teeming with buffalo, and hunting prowess became the most valued trait. The result was that as a man lost his skill, so he lost his prestige. The Tanala of Madagascar grow rice by a method which requires a great deal of collaboration, and you have large families of men living together on a basis of sharing; their neighbours, the Betsiles, grow rice by a method which does not require such a co-operative labour force, and you have a system of private property and a mass of landless workers. With our advanced techniques and lines of communication, we are not so dependent, save in time of war, on our immediate environment; but the predicament of our own country at the present moment, with our island protection practically lost, with our population of fifty million to feed, and our close proximity to the Continent, provides a forceful example of the significance of geography. One has only to think of the siting of cities, the uneven dispersal of mineral resources, which has even endowed the South Pole with a belated popularity, and the part played by rivers and mountains as links and barriers, to appreciate the importance of geography to the sociologist.

I have tried in this chapter to elaborate the field with which the social scientist is concerned. My task in the next and in the penultimate chapter is to consider in what ways and to what parts of the field he can profitably devote his attention in a manner which can reasonably be called scientific.

CHAPTER III

The Scientific Approach

I WANT now to consider the scientific approach to the vast field of inquiry to which I have already referred. It may well be that from the heights of physical science the social scientists look more like a group of rag-pickers haphazardly grubbing about among a pile of human refuse than serious scientists engaged in the co-operative construction of a systematic body of knowledge. And it must be confessed that when one reviews the books that have been published, the papers issued in journals of sociology and social psychology, and the stream of MA, MSc, and PhD theses over a relatively short space of time, it is difficult to reduce them to any order at all. All the same, the social scientist may be excused a gesture of impatience if the physical scientist twits him about the undeveloped and disorderly state of affairs in his field, because the most singular thing about the physical scientist is that when he leaves the heights and comes down into the social world—which he often does at lunch time—his generalizations, his pronouncements, his laying down of the law, often go to show that he has left behind him that demand for accuracy and evidence upon which his own majestic edifice has been built.

The appearance of disorder to which I have referred is, I think, due to a variety of factors. In the first place, the field of investigation is indefinitely varied; secondly, the nature of one of the agreed tests of plausibility does not require the establishment of a theoretical framework;

thirdly, the subject-matter is difficult to handle, partly because of its very familiarity; fourthly, the work of social scientists is more closely bound up with the practical frame of reference of contemporary problems than is the case with physical scientists; and fifthly, the social scientist is limited in his investigations by the opportunities offered to him. All these factors tend to make the empirical research of social scientists varied, unrelated the one to the other, and frequently unconnected with social theory. I do not say that this is bad or good; it seems to me to be inevitable from the nature of the subject.

The first factor I have mentioned—the variety in the field of social action—needs no comment. Professor Lasswell investigates the sociology of politics; Professor Sargant Florence the relation between investments, location, and size of plant; the London School of Economics has in hand a vast project concerned with the nature of social class and the degree of mobility in it; while in Liverpool they have been engaged in research into the social relations in hospitals. One could obviously extend the list indefinitely. This merely means that in the total field of human interaction some social scientists dip here and some there, and there is no particular reason why the research of one will have any bearing on the research of another, though of course it sometimes does.

The second factor is, I think, more significant. Social science must follow the same pattern of inference as any other science. A problem presents itself, an hypothesis suggests itself, deductions are drawn, verification or falsification ensues. This is, of course, deceptively simple. What is a problem will depend, as we shall see, on the general climate of opinion and interest—in Professor Popper's language, on the *horizon of expectations* prevalent at the time. The hypothesis may be derived from a relatively compact body of accepted theory; it may be a sudden hunch, it may be a vague and unspoken rejection of certain logically possible factors; it may be rendered precise before or during the research. Verification may be—and in the social sciences frequently is—difficult, but verification must be in principle, if not in fact, possible, otherwise the seeming hypothesis is no hypothesis at all. The hypothesis itself may be an elaborate system of deductively related propositions or it may be a generalization of the form : " whenever you have x you have y." The latter is unsatisfying until it is so related to an hypothesis of the former type—what we call a " theory "—that it can be deducible from it.

Now, in the social sciences there are, I think, two rather amorphous bodies of theory from which hypotheses are derived, and in terms of which explanations are found to be satisfying. I will distinguish them by the names " psychological theory " and " social theory." The former is concerned with what human beings are like, the latter with what is likely to happen when human beings in large or small numbers interact with one another. This distinction is a real one in practice, but ultimately untenable, because what people are like depends on their social contacts, and what happens when they interact depends on what people are like. Nevertheless there are, at the present juncture of social science, two attitudes of research, or two standards of satisfyingness.

Let us take an example. In a recent issue of the *British Journal of Sociology* (Vol. II, p. 105) Dr Eisenstadt reports on his researches into Youth Culture and Social Structure in Israel. It appears that in some communities in Israel there are active youth organizations, in some not. Why? Dr Eisenstadt does not tell us anything about the heights or weights of Israeli youth—he considers the matter irrelevant. Doubtless without explicitly rejecting a host of such logically possible cause factors, he notes that: " a specific youth culture is most developed among the different professional, bureaucratic, middle-class and upper working-class sections of the urban population, in the communal settlements (Kibutzim), and among those sections of the Oriental Jews which are going through rapid processes of 'culture contact ' and culture change. It is least developed among those Oriental families which still persist in their traditional setting, in the co-operative settlements (Moshar Ordim, which is a co-operative village consisting of family farms), . . . and among some of the lower urban classes." His eye is caught by some differences likely on general social-psychological grounds—differences in social contacts. But still: Why ? What is the difference between these two types of social life ? Very briefly Dr Eisenstadt argues that where a boy or a girl is brought up in a close family circle to do at an early age what they will do when grown up, so that there is no discontinuity between childhood, adolescence, and adulthood, they do not *need* to develop a youth culture. Where you have either a separation of children from the family circle so that they live apart, feed apart, and learn apart, or where you have a long period of training for some distant specialized job, then you have a discontinuity between the family and the total social structure into which the youths are to be absorbed. So they form a world or " culture " of their own. " Through participation in the youth culture the child and adolescent gets some compensation for some of the social experience denied to him in the adult world " such as " acquisition of full status and recognition as an independent individual, and the attainment of not too-distant gratification and working for achievable goals." Such an explanation is plausible. " Yes," we say, " if they feel out of things, they may well collect together so as to have something they can be ' in '." The psychological theory is obvious :

everyone wants to be thought something of and will do something about it if this desire is not satisfied. These young people were in a position in which they were not thought much of, and bolstering each other up is a way of doing something about it. And so we may leave the matter. Now I am not saying that this piece of research has no bearing on social theory; it has. It suggests the hypothesis: in any social structure which deprives any of its participants of what is *de facto* adequate recognition of status, differentiation will occur which will compensate for such deprivation. It suggests, indeed, a number of hypotheses about the general problem of discontinuity in entering adult life, a problem to which Ruth Benedict has made an interesting contribution.[1] My point is, however, that we can be satisfied with the psychological interpretation without necessarily linking it up with social theory. Psychological interpretation is, as it were, a satisfactory half-way house.

Again, take Professor Sargant Florence's [2] investigation into the control and policy of large-scale British industrial joint-stock companies. He finds great variety in their structure and expects the variety to be reflected in their policies; and he goes on to say that " the plausible working hypotheses to be tested are mainly drawn from introspective psychology and from economics with its presumption that men want a maximum and/or a secure income plus some power, fame or reputation in the community." And if his hypotheses are not falsified we shall be satisfied with their psychological plausibility within the economic context to which they apply. He does, to be sure, relate his research " to all large-scale organizations, governmental, commercial, ecclesiastical, educational, military "—but that, if I am not mistaken, is not the prime concern.

[1] *Personality* (ed. Kluckholm and Murray ; Cape, 1949), p. 414.
[2] *Brit. J. of Sociol.*, Vol. I, 1950, p. 234.

The point I am trying to make may be put in this way: you might have a science in which you have a body of theory and all research might either be dictated by it or converge on to it; or you might have a body of theory which is a specialist study to which actual research makes only incidental contributions, while the research itself is to a very large extent carried on without reference to the body of theory, finding its validation at the court of what we might call sophisticated common sense. The latter is the case with the social sciences. An acceptable answer to the question " why ? " is found in terms of human nature, and therefore it is not necessary to pursue the matter further and see how the research contributes to building social theory. The result of this, again, is a widely dispersed and unrelated coagulation of empirical investigations.

My third factor which contributes to the lack of order in the social sciences is not easy to express. It may be approached by saying that the word " science " in the expression " social science " has to be more generously interpreted than it need be in the case of the advanced physical sciences. By this I mean that the very minimum of its meaning—unbiased observation and respect for evidence—is significant. The position is that socio-logical thought is only beginning to extricate itself from the common-sensical sociological assumptions of everyone in general and of the administrator in particular. These are saturated with prejudices, approval, and disapproval, and it is not easy even to achieve what Merton calls a " general sociological orientation." However, granted that we have achieved sociological orientation, we find ourselves equipped with imprecise and misleading concepts and an enormous ignorance about the social world around us. This means that an unusual amount of thought has to be given to analysis and the refinement of our conceptual tools. We think we know what marriage is, what the State is, what crime is, what class is, and so on. We even think that we have to investigate the " true nature " of marriage, State, crime, class, or whatever notion is before us; such is the misleading nature of language and that false proposition that " nouns are the names of things." We discover that we have to divest ourselves of our preconceived notions, take up a new position, and examine what detectable social interactions and restrictions are sufficiently distinctive for us to use such a word as " marriage " of them; what decision-making is implied by the word " State "; what criterion of deviance is implied by the word " crime "—and what is excluded as coming more appropriately under the heading of " unsuccessful reform," or permitted revolutionary activity; what marks of prestige or power distinguish one class from another. All this theoretical work is essential, and has a direct bearing on empirical research, because unless you have a clear idea as to how to identify the items which you are going to investigate, your research will not be repeatable. Equipped with adequate conceptual tools we advance upon our ignorance. We may have a clear idea of marriage in this culture—but how many women get married and at what ages ? We may have an idea about the political structure of decision-making, but who are the decision-makers ? What is their social background—a topic investigated recently by W. L. Guttsman,[1] who pointed out the significance of political experience before achieving cabinet rank, which tends to limit achievement to those who can get the experience. If we define crime as action contravening the law and start examining business conduct, at any rate in America, we find—if Edwin H. Sutherland is right—that " the theories of the criminologists that crime is due to poverty or to psychopathic and socio-pathic conditions statistically associated with poverty are

[1] *Brit. J. of Sociol.*, Vol. II, 1951, p. 122.

invalid because they are derived from samples which are grossly biased with respect to socio-economic status." [1] And when it comes to social class, a matter about which many of us feel competent to speak without any investigation whatever, we find that it is an elusive concept, varying in its meaning from group to group and extremely difficult to get any precise information about at all. The outcome of our ignorance about what goes on around us, when we have become aware of it, has been that a considerable amount of research is pure fact-finding and nothing else.

This descriptive type of research, which is sometimes looked down on, is as essential as conceptual analysis. Of course a great deal of fact-finding is done by government departments, and now that the Government intervenes more and more in our domestic and economic activities, more and more information is available in that indispensable compilation: the *Annual Abstract of Statistics*. These, however, are seldom complete enough for our purposes, and one of the jobs of the social scientist is to persuade the authorities, who alone have the means at their disposal for the collecting of data on a nation-wide basis, to ask questions to which he wants to know the answer. Again, the statistical information itself has to be examined, sifted, and ordered so that the maximum amount of information can be got out of it: I need only remind you of Carr-Saunders and Caradog Jones's *Social Structure of England and Wales*,[2] of Hermann Mannheim's work on criminal statistics, and of the work of the Oxford Institute of Statistics on the distribution of incomes and property,[3 and 4] as a few examples of researches of this kind.

[1] *Social Analysis*, ed. by Wilson and Kolb (Harcourt Brace, 1949), p. 796.
[2] OUP, 1937.
[3] *Levelling of Incomes Since 1938*, by D. Seers (Blackwell n.d.).
[4] " Distribution of Capital in Private Hands," by K. M. Langley, *OUP Bulletin of Statistics*, Vol. 12 (1950), p. 339; Vol. 13 (1951), p. 351.

Another difficulty which confronts the social scientist is the methodological problem. It is all very well to be sociologically oriented, but the problem always is: how to go about your investigations? Quite apart from the problems of sampling, and the assessment of results by the application of statistical criteria which are now becoming routine considerations, though sometimes one finds a disastrous neglect of such matters by people who ought to know better [I think of Rowntree and Laver's book on *English Life and Leisure* (Longmans, 1951)], there are the far more formidable problems of what Professor Simey calls " getting in, staying in, and getting out." How can one get one's information without disturbing what one is investigating? And what information can one get that is relevant to one's purposes? And what—to use Professor Sargant Florence's expression—" para-statistical indices " can one devise for measurement? I think, for instance, of the alternatives of open-ended or " formal " questionnaires, participant observation, and the oblique approach of a research worker who pretended that he was interested in finding out whether the inhabitants of Bethnal Green wanted to move to a new town, while he really wanted to find out whether they were anti-Semitic. I think also of Dr Dennis Chapman's attempt to develop a scale of measurement of economic status by means of an assessment of household equipment, similar to the scale developed in America by Chapin, according to which a library table scores eight, a piano bench (not chair or stool) scores four, while two marks are taken off for a sewing machine in the wrong place and for the presence of an alarm clock. " Windows with drapes " on the other hand entitle their owners to an additional two marks. All this means that a great deal of research is significant not only—even not so much—because of the results, but rather because of the method used. Indeed, much attitude-research is carried out in America on university students—an ever-available collection of guinea-pigs in that country—simply for methodological purposes. And Professor Madge's [1] investigation into family budgets and the way they reveal family decision-making is, as I think he would agree, in part a methodological inquiry, though of course the results will no doubt be illuminating in their own right.

The very nature of social research—its novelty, its need for basic information, and its difficulty—means that a great deal of it is analytical, fact-finding of all kinds, and devised to test out new methods. This, again, makes for variety.

The fourth factor I described as the close connection that social science has with practical everyday affairs. The social scientist himself is interested in the world about him in a practical everyday sense as well as in a remoter purely scientific sense, and this means that the topics he will investigate will reflect what one might call the " climate of interest " in which he is operating. This, in turn, will partly determine the topics which he will investigate—again making for variety and lack of order. Some of his investigations are operational, in the sense of providing the executive with an analytical and objective basis for decisions, to which I would add the investigation into the effects of policy. Here we have research into the facts, demographic and economic, with which the administrator has to deal, and which provide what has been called the " logic of the situation." The social scientists in Dortmund and Munster are mainly engaged in providing a factual basis for reconstruction and for agrarian reform in Westphalia, and for the housing of refugees from the Eastern Zone of Germany. Here, too, we have those numerous social surveys, so many of which have been directed in whole or in part by the University of Birmingham.

[1] Professor Madge kindly showed me a preliminary report on his project.

The topic of social surveys is of further interest as illustrating the change in approach which has accompanied a change of emphasis from the alignment of streets to the people who live in them. I am not going to attempt to trace in detail the history of town planning from the age of sewage to the age of neighbourhood units. I suppose it starts with the early slum-agitation of the 1840s, which existed side by side with planning residential areas for the well-to-do. It was impeded by the demands for economy. "The social reformer in office," wrote a contributor to the *Financial Reformer* in August 1858, "is a dangerously popular man; because he is in many cases a dishonest one. . . . His political science is the science of guiding the sewage of the country in the way it should go . . . it is the science of improving the architectural aspect of a city until it takes a foremost rank in the note-book of the dilettante tourist . . . but it is not the science of good, cheap and honest government, which alone can make a country great and respected and a people really happy and prosperous." Then there were the societies for rehousing the poor and the Torrens and Cross Acts of 1868 and 1875. Gradually the size of cities and the development of suburbs brought about a more general preoccupation with the city as a whole, with general amenities rather than the mere cleansing of the poor. And so we come on to the garden city—it was " urgently necessary," so ran the prospectus for Welwyn, "that a convincing demonstration should be given of some more scientific method than has hitherto prevailed of providing for the expansion of the industries and population of Greater London." It was largely a matter of amenities, of siting, of traffic regulation—in short, of the apparatus of living. Not that the people were entirely neglected. In 1846 James Silk Buckingham said that men living in villages or in the open areas of large towns were better than men

living in " a crowded and crooked-lane neighbourhood "
because " if a man did wrong under such circumstances,
no one would speak to him; he would find the place
insupportable and would be compelled to go away "—
where to is not indicated. And in the amenity town
planning, the movements of the population were noted
as a guide to convenient siting.

But nowadays the neighbourhood unit is the bone of
contention. Psychological assumptions, often ill supported by evidence, are made, and the modern social
scientist in the field of social surveys directs his attention
to the daily life of the inhabitants. Thus in the Pilot
Survey of Oxford Dr Mogey notes a " significant
correlation between maladjustment in the home and
acceptance of neighbours " [1]; W. Watson [2] tells us that in
Buckhaven " the fact that the back-courts form the play
space for association forced into rival groups certain
children whose homes were separated only by the
breadth of the street, for the children are orientated
towards the backs of the houses, and the street with the
front doors facing one another is a kind of no-man's-
land "; while other investigations have brought into
prominence the social consequences when the back-doors
of adjacent houses face one another. The operational
world of the administrator and the social scientist has
been extended to include face-to-face social action, and
not only in town planning, but in industrial, economic,
and political planning as well.

Policy testing, too, is bound to be topical. Investigations have been carried out by the Acton Society into the
effects of nationalization on the coal industry; investigations are demanded into the working of the Health
Service; an American social scientist has recently been

[1] Quoted by permission of Dr J. M. Mogey.
[2] Quoted by permission from an unpublished thesis entitled " Children
in a Mining Community," p. 74.

engaged in a study of joint consultations in Great Britain; and a German social scientist has been inquiring into the dispute about the nationalization of the iron and steel industry. Operational research is closely connected with policy making and policy testing; but topicality as a factor directing research to one problem rather than another is not confined to this. The elections of 1945 and 1950 have given rise to numerous inquiries, including that sponsored by the Nuffield Foundation, into voting behaviour. Delinquency is a pressing problem, and the dispersal of television sets and the possible effects of viewing are being studied by the Audience Research Department of the BBC. Old age in our present demographic and economic situation is of special interest; accordingly we have an experimental approach made to *Skill and Age*[1] and a survey of *Older People and their Employment*.[2]

Again, there are new developments which offer a quasi-experimental situation to explore. Much of great interest, to which I shall refer later, is coming out of Israel. Let us hope that some research will be set afoot to study the dramatic changes that are going on in China.

Then there is what I might call the episodic study: the study of some incident of interest. This may be illustrated by Durward Pruden's study[3] of a Texas lynching; by William Gremley's study[4] of a riot in Cicero when a negro moved into an area mainly inhabited by Czechs who feared the consequent decline in property value; by Paterson's study[5] of a strike in the Lanarkshire coalfield; and, if we may include among the episodic, the unusual, by S. M. Lipset's study[6] of agricultural socialism

[1] *Nuffield Foundation*, by A. T. Welford *et al.* (OUP, 1951).
[2] *Social Survey*, by G. Thomas and B. Osborne (Central Office of Information, 1951).
[3] *Sociological Analysis*, ed. by Wilson and Kolb (1949), p. 335.
[4] *Brit. J. of Sociol.*, Vol. III (1952), p. 322.
[5] *Sociological Review*, Vol. XLIII (1951), p. 57.
[6] *Agrarian Socialism* (University of California Press, 1950).

in Saskatchewan; and by the same author's description of a democratically organized trade union in America, in which the iron law of oligarchy is corrected by an internal party system.[1]

And finally research is bound to be directed into channels of availability. How often we say about a problem: It ought to be investigated; why is there no research project? How often we should be floored if someone were to offer us the money to do the research! One of the reasons why the student population, schoolchildren, delinquents, and the poor have had so much attention is undoubtedly the fact that they are accessible. We know scarcely anything of statistical value about the lives of the rich, or the upper middle classes, because we dare not knock at their front doors. The diet of dustmen can be discovered with ease; the junketing of judges is wrapped in obscurity.

So far I have attempted to give reasons for the dispersal and uncoordinated activities of social scientists. They are all engaged in studying some aspect of human interaction or of its resultants. The topics to which they devote their minds are spread wide over an enormous field; they are dictated partly by the present condition of the science, partly by their interest and training, partly by the current climate of interest, partly by what happens to crop up, and partly by the chances open to them. I have not mentioned the lack of money for financing their researches, because it is a topic too familiar and too distressing to dwell upon. No wonder social science is an unorganized hodge-podge of endeavours. No wonder research from America is so often of no interest to us in England because of the absence in a great deal of it of any contribution to social theory. Not that I think it ought not to be done, though I think that people engaged in research might sometimes be encouraged to see their

[1] *Brit. J. of Sociol.*, Vol. III (1952), p. 47.

researches in a somewhat wider perspective, to ask themselves about their bearing on more general issues. One hopes, of course, that it will all come in somehow in the end, but unless we can devise some cheap method of publication or some efficient method of registration, a great deal of research, too long perhaps for publication in journals, may well rot in the cellars of university libraries.

I have dealt with the contribution (or lack of it) which pieces of research can (or do not) make to social theory; now I must turn to this complex subject.

Everyone, social scientists included, has a vague conception of the society in which he lives, the various groupings within it, and of other societies outside with which his own has contacts. The conceptions vary in complexity and in comprehension, roughly according to range of participation, interest, and communicated knowledge which characterize the holders of them. The range and complexity of the conceptual structure used by the administrator are obviously greater, because he requires a greater scope for his activity than that, say, of a crofter on the Isle of Arran. The sociologist, as I have already said, aims at making his own conceptual structure more precise, and to communicate such increased precision to the administrator.

The theoretically-minded sociologist, however, has something else in view. He wants to construct what I have called a working model, expressed in a system of propositions in terms of which he can interpret and predict social action and its resultant consequences, and from which the various regularities which have been found by empirical research to hold with some degree of probability could be deduced. Alas, the cupboard is bare. " Despite the many volumes dealing with the history of sociological theory," writes R. K. Merton,[1] " and despite the plethora of empirical investigations,

[1] *Social Theory and Social Structure* (Free Press, 1951), p. 92.

sociologists may discuss the logical criteria of sociological laws without citing a single instance which fully
satisfies these criteria." We have, no doubt, innumer-
able explanations which satisfy us on what I may call the
psychological level; but, expressed as sociological rules,
they have very limited application. Any explanation by
its logical form implies rules, even if there is only one
case in the world which fulfils the conditions for their
application; but I can think of no well-established rule
which will hold for all social systems. What we have is a
multiplicity of what might be called " culture-bound "
rules, i.e. rules which apply, say, in the American world,
but not here; rules which apply under capitalism but
not under socialism; rules which apply to the children
of immigrants in Jerusalem, but not to the children of
the citizens of Birmingham.

The problem of voting in this country and in America
is vastly different from the problem of voting in Egypt,
as revealed by a recent investigation,[1] where we are told
that " one is not surprised to find that no elaborate
electioneering campaign is required to persuade the S'Afra
villagers to vote for the candidate who belongs to their
stock. In fact the candidate for Silwa constituency has
won the last three elections with a sweeping majority,
irrespective of the political views of his opponents. The
rule is that the people of Silwa should vote for their
' paternal cousin '! "

The rules are relatively simple or relatively sophisticated generalizations about human conduct applied to
certain circumstances; the more specific the circum-
stance, or " initial conditions," to use a fashionable
phrase, the narrower the application.

But though there is no established body of social
theory, we can consider the kind of thing that would be

[1] *A Study of Growing Up in an Egyptian Community*, by H. M. Ammar
(PhD Thesis, 1952; London University).

meant by it. We have social interaction at the face-to-face level, and we have relatively large numbers of human beings interacting indirectly; these latter units we have in mind when we speak of inclusive societies (a notion which could, I think, be operationally defined in terms of interaction at the face-to-face level in chain reaction and at the administrative level). We agree that in such societies changes in one aspect are likely to cause changes elsewhere. This happens when the initial change alters the stage upon which other interactions take place. Parents do not beget so many children, there are not enough of them to fill the industrial roles, the stage is altered, and old men of sixty-five look different—they are potential sources of labour. We can, no doubt, follow such chains of causation from one set of interactions to another within the same system. We conceive of the system as a kind of linked area throughout which repercussions range. But sociologists have been haunted by another conception. It is the conception of society as an organism with self-regulating tendencies—the conception, if you like, of society as a machine kept in order by negative feed-back.

We all know that we must not speak of society as an organism: the ambiguities are dangerous; but all the same the concept for which that dubious word was used is with us when we talk about understanding society as a whole, when we talk about cohesion, continuity, equilibrium, solidarity, and—most used of all words—integration. "We speak," says S. F. Nadel,[1] " of these states as of ' necessities ' of group existence; others would speak of ' forces ' of integration, as though there existed something in society actively pressing for greater unity." "Whichever phrase is used," he goes on, " it means the same thing, namely observed processes

[1] *Foundation of Social Anthropology*, by Cohen and West (OUP, 1951), p. 371.

leading to smooth, and full co-adaptation of behaviour; control of friction and conflicts; the preservation of unity. Now these are all *attributes of society as we can alone conceive it*. In calling these ' forces ' or ' necessities ' a ' function ' we merely translate statements about just-so existence into statements about a goal or purpose in this existence. For society *means* integration and the rest is some form of degree." And this is implied by Radcliffe-Brown [1] when he says: " The function of a particular social usage is the contribution it makes to the *total social life* as the functioning of the *total social system*. Such a view implies that a social system has a certain kind of unity, which we may speak of as a functional unity." Such a view is implied by Merton's notion of latent functions, in so far as such behaviour unintentionally, but *de facto*, preserves integration. Such is the view of those who say that our *malaise* is due to a lack of integration in society.

Whether the functionalist view can be applied to large-scale society to the same purpose as it has been applied to the simpler peoples is a matter of question. I agree with Merton's doubts.[2] There are items which may be said to be functional for some members of a society but not for all; there are items which may be of functional value to a few but disfunctional to the many: the cosh, for example. We must be prepared for a certain loose-ness in our large-scale integration, the admission of much diversity without impairing the degree of co-hesiveness.

Now, such a conception implies, I think, a set of psychological hypotheses, such as: (1) Human beings enjoy smooth social interaction and seek to ensure it and to perpetuate it. (2) They tend to resist change, preferring some (unspecified) degree of discomfort to a

[1] *Andaman Islanders* (Free Press, 1948), p. 397.
[2] *Social Theory and Social Structure* (Free Press, 1951), Chap. I.

certain (unspecified) degree of alteration. (3) Where change threatens disruption they will tend first to compensate for it in some way or another, psychological or institutional. These are very rough indications, but I think they are required—and there may be more—if we are to devise rules of integration from the rules of social action. But the concept of integration is useless unless it helps us to understand and predict social change. This involves knowing (a) the level of aspiration and interaction at which men are prepared to take steps (" For," as Hobbes observed, " as long as a man thinketh himself well . . . it is impossible for him to desire the change thereof, and even though discontented, he will not show it if there is no just cause for making the government responsible." Hobbes, of course, was thinking of revolution, which is only one form of social change, but his remarks have an aptness here) ; and (b) we want to know what steps—if I may call them so, for they may well be unconsciously motivated—he will be likely to take (i) at this or that measurable degree of discomfort; (ii) in this or that type of social context; and (iii) we want a method of measuring integration, or cohesion, or whatever term we choose to use; and this means a more precise definition of integration than we yet have.

Now all this is a very tall order. If we could achieve the establishment of such rules of integration we should be able to go to a society and say : " This society has such and such a degree of integration; the institutional and belief structure is so and so; the degree of tension here is this, and there is that; according to the rules there will be rebellion here, a crop of neuroses there, the formation of sub-groups here, the formulation of compensatory myths there." We might also, presumably, have appropriate recipes. Expressed in this way it may sound somewhat absurd, but this is undoubtedly the kind of thing that the sociologist would like. It is the kind of thinking that crops up—not in these terms, of course— all over the place. The Marxists are interested in, and, indeed, have thrown light upon the "revolutionary situation," a degree of disintegration at which a complete change is likely to occur; Dr Alex Comfort, to name but one of many, thinks that integration can be achieved only in small groups; this, too, was Durkheim's own view. It is well, I think, that we should consider, however sketchily, what is implied by the ideal of a social theory, because I do not think that writers who use its concepts always realize what is involved. To establish it research would have to be directed towards the methodological problem of measurement and the analytical problem of definition. It would have to work out the implication of integration and state its hypotheses in such terms. And such research as has been carried out would have to be sifted for the light which it throws upon the main theoretical problems.

Of course such a body of theoretical rules would be highly abstract. *What* pressures and tensions exist are only empirically discoverable; what possibilities of adjustment lie open, again, are to be discovered only by inspection. What we should have established would be certain general rules of adaptation or compensation which could be applied to all cases, but which would lead to different inferences from case to case. In fact we should have a set of social rules, which have " a society " as their logical subject, functioning much as do the general psychological rules in a great deal of social research today.

And now, at the end of it all, we must ask whether we are on a wild-goose chase. This, I think, is a question which cannot be answered as yet. If it is a wild-goose chase, then—if I may be permitted a quite scandalous mixture of metaphor—the ghost of integration as a force must be laid. It may be that there is no sensible sense in which we can speak of anything like a " process making for cohesion " or a " force of integration." It may be that the hypothesis of dynamic integration is fruitless. We cannot yet know. Meanwhile, in view of the various (often tacit) assumptions that are so frequently made, the problem must be investigated. If what I should like to call the " integration hypothesis " proves fruitless, then in *that* sense of social theory there is no social theory. And now, where are we ? Back, I would say, at the psychological level. Social theory would now mean that while there is nothing that could profitably be called a " force " holding societies together at all convenient costs, it is nevertheless important to have due regard to social factors : agreed beliefs, demographic data, and the like. Research in one society would still be relevant to research in another, provided the conditions were comparable. Youth in Israel may be significant for youth in England if the circumstances are similar, but there would be no overriding rules to apply. Which of these alternatives will prove the more satisfactory I do not know. Nor, indeed, does anyone else.

CHAPTER IV

The Small Group

I PROPOSE to divide this chapter into four unequal parts which I shall call: the sociometric, the field theory, the therapeutic, and the analytical approaches.

Sociometry is an attempt to establish an index of social intercourse. It originated with the work of Moreno in Vienna and in the United States. It is a very simple technique. Given a group, you ask each member of it such questions as: With whom would you like to share a room? To whom would you like to work next? With whom would you like to spend your leisure time? The questions are dictated by the pursuits of the group you are investigating. You may allow one, or two, or three, or even four choices. You can then calculate who gets most choices, who gets least choices, and who gets no choices, and what mutual choices are made. An attempt has been made by Uric Bronfenbrenner [1] to standardize a scale applicable to a limited number of participants using up to four choices on a limited number of criteria. Anyway, one can calculate the number of choices on any criterion and then see how they are distributed. The pattern of choice can also be made clearer by mapping them out on a sociogram, as it is called, where lines are drawn from one member to another indicating choice, reciprocated or not. The estimation of social interaction can also be made more complicated by introducing negative criteria: With whom would you like least (or positively dislike)

[1] *Sociometry*, Vol. VII, (1944).

working ? And now for its value. In the first place, it may be used for therapeutic purposes to pick out what are known as " isolates," and this, indeed, is one of the uses to which Moreno put it in his work at the Training School for girls at Hudson, New York, which was a kind of approved school for delinquent girls. However, more can be got out of the sociogram than that. It reveals the stars, the popular choices with lines drawn towards them from many quarters, the cliques who choose one another but choose no one else, the chain of influence, which often shows that the popular are by no means always the most influential: to be influential you must occupy a key position in a system of chains through which you can make your influence felt. It also reveals networks along which rumour runs and, so Moreno found at Hudson, channels of what we might call " delinquescence "—plots to run away and the like. Moreno's general argument is, very roughly, this: People have the capacity for spontaneous affection and friendship; this gets twisted and inhibited in the course of life, and leads to withdrawal and disharmony. In the case of his delinquent girls, therefore, it was important that they should be grouped in the separate cottages, of which the institution was composed, in such a way as to give scope for such spontaneity as they had; it was therefore important that girls who liked one another should be together and that " isolates " or " neglectees " should be placed where they would be less isolated and less neglected. Accordingly he tried to re-shuffle the girls at Hudson so as to produce the maximum ' intro-version,' as he rather unhappily calls it, where most choices are made within the group and not to outsiders. New intakes were placed, after an elaborate set of interviews, with companions and under the house-mother of their choice. In his book, *Who Shall Survive?*,[1] where the

[1] Beacon House, 1934.

theory and the technique are described, he shows some evidence that such planned placing led to more harmonious living, as indeed we should expect, and also was of therapeutic value. This therapeutic value of harmonious group-living we shall meet with again.

The stress laid by Moreno on " spontaneity " and its inhibitions is the basis for two other techniques with which I shall not deal in any detail: the " psychodrama " and the " socio-drama." Patients, for we must now call them such, who find human relations difficult are invited to act out scenes in which they are called upon to display emotions, either associated with their own difficulties—such as a feeling of persecution or of being " picked on "—or simply as an exercise in expression. In the socio-drama they take " roles " of a social nature and act out these: this technique has also been used to train people for certain social positions, such, for instance, as that of foremen.

In the Hudson institution, as I have said, the emphasis lay on individual rehabilitation through membership of a congenial group. In many other uses of sociometry the emphasis lies rather on the morale and solidarity of the group itself. It was found, for instance, that two American air crews in the last war differed markedly in their morale. A sociometric index was applied in which the criteria were: With whom would you like to fly ? With whom would you dislike to fly ? In the air crew that had the higher morale almost all the choices were internal, and many were directed towards the flying officer and his lieutenant. In the one which had the lower morale no choices at all, but rather rejections, were directed to the leader, many choices went outside the team, and such as were within revealed cliques of mutual choices.

Another field in which sociometry has been used, together with other tests, is the field of co-operative enterprises. H. F. Infield made an interesting comparison of two co-operative communities: Matador and Macedonia. The former was a group of fifteen war veterans in Saskatchewan; the latter a group of fifteen conscientious objectors settled in Georgia. Matador was a completely male population most of whom were brought up as farmers, and half of them had joined the community mainly from economic motives. Macedonia was a mixed population of three bachelors, six married couples and their five children, coming from various walks of life, some of them having been farmers, and joining the community from predominantly ideological motives. Several criteria were used: Working together? Talking over personal problems? Visiting sports and social affairs? (Matador). And: Visiting at meals and for an evening? (Macedonia). These two last were grouped together as " leisure time." There were other criteria, but in order to use the Bronfenbrenner scale, which works for only three criteria, these three were picked out. Attention was now concentrated on *mutual* choices, and here the two groups differed. In Matador on the work criterion there were ten mutual choices, and only two members participated in *no* mutual choice; while in Macedonia there were seven mutual choices and five participated in no mutual choice. On leisure time, in Matador, there were seven mutual choices, in Macedonia nine; on personal problems, on intimacy one might say, in Matador there were only five mutual choices; in Macedonia eight. Assuming that mutual choices give some indication of mutuality, one can appreciate Infield's conclusion that: " While Matador is quite well teamed up for work, Macedonia for one reason or another appears to be weakest on this point. But while at Matador there is only fair mutuality in leisure-time activities, and only relatively little personal confidence, Macedonia, in spite of sex cleavage, shows a high degree of mutual confidence among its members and an almost optimal amount of mutuality in leisure-time activities." [1] From which he infers that " if the living standards . . . should sink below a certain minimal level, the personal ties would prove too weak in the case of Matador to hold the group together. Macedonia on the other hand would have a much better chance of survival even under conditions which would appear to the Matador group as unbearable." [2]

A stress on work was a weakness in a manufacturing co-operative in Clermont, France. [3] There were one hundred men and fifteen women working in a factory producing metal parts, while sixty-three women, who were connected by marriage with the productive members, belonged to the group as a whole. In this case, in addition to sociometric tests, questionnaires were used which aimed at an assessment of " co-operative potential," as Infield calls it, and their views about what they missed in the community. The criteria used were the same as in the Matador and Macedonia study. Among the productive members there were no fewer than seventy-eight " neglectees " who got from one to five choices, and nine " isolates "; while among the sixty-three family companions there were fifty-two " neglectees " and seven " isolates." The " co-operative potential " test, for what it is worth, indicates a higher readiness to co-operate than was in fact shown. Now the whole point of this group was that " work was to remain subordinated to the pursuit of the industrial worker's need for social reintegration, with all that this implies in terms of sense of belonging." The *groupe de quartier*, or neighbourhood

[1] *Co-operative Group Living*, by H. F. Infield and J. B. Maier (Ed.) (Henry Kooris & Co, 1950), p. 218.

[2] "The Use of the Sociometric Test in Co-operative Community Research," *Proc. of the XIV International Congress of Sociology*, Vol. III, p. 12.

[3] *Co-operative Living*, Vol. III, No. 2, 1951, p. 1.

group, was essential to the enterprise. The investigation showed that this aspect was a failure. Of the thirty-eight *mutual* choices among the companions, twenty-four were made on the criterion of work, and among the family companions all the fourteen mutual choices were confined to work. Furthermore, those who were popular were those who, on the whole, scored low for co-operativeness, while those who were co-operative-minded did not get many choices. In fact they had been concentrating on economic success rather than social integration and had, it was suspected, accepted new members for their technical skill rather than for other personal qualifications.

Now in these three cases—Matador, Macedonia, and Clermont—the results are not surprising; but it is argued that sociometry reveals more clearly defects that one suspects, and points more precisely to what is wrong. Other examples could be given of the application of sociometry to the planning of resettlement communities : the study by Loomis [1] of a Mexican village, and the evaluation of Jewish training farms which prepare their members for life on a Kvutza.[2, 3]

However, enough has been said to give you an idea of sociometry, and I turn now to field theory. This approach is based on the work of Kurt Lewin. I find some difficulty in doing it justice because I am not satisfied about its value. Indeed, I would not allow its celebrity to stand in the way of its omission. I mention it because of two pieces of research which are certainly of interest, and which field theorists claim to be unintelligible without the theory. The theory itself is an application of

[1] " Informal Grouping in a Spanish-American Village," *Sociometry*, Vol. 4, p. 36.

[2] H. F. Infield, *Co-operative Living*, Vol. II, p. 1.

[3] Examples of the use of sociometric methods in educational psychology will be found in *Studies in the Social Psychology of Adolescence*, ed. C. M. Fleming (Kegan Paul, 1951).

certain concepts of physics and topology to actions in a situation. The situation is a field of forces. Its content must be understood psychologically as well as physically. A child is in a room and there is a sweet on the mantelpiece. The physical sweet is important only if it has value for the child; the child's ambition will be determined partly by the presence of the sweet before its very eyes, and partly by its internal physiological condition, which has, of course, a past history about sweets behind it. A vector of force pushes the child towards the sweet, which is said to have positive valence. Suppose there is a ban on sweet-eating, suppose a door is ajar and therefore an area of visibility from the outer world. We now have a more complex field: positive vectors push the child towards the sweet, negative vectors repel from the sweet—the fear of punishment; and from the area of visibility—the fear of being seen. The child is propelled towards the danger zone. In this new region the repelling force is stronger, the conflict of forces has changed; the child accordingly, as we should say, hesitates. If the positive vector is strong enough the child will move, or be moved, into the danger zone. Now a new situation is present with the positive value of the sweet having added to *it* the positive values of the further area of invisibility. The child darts across. And in the new region the conflict continues: the stronger force wins and the child gets the sweet, flies from temptation, or stands transfixed in doubt. This is a simple example. The forces are symbolized in a very professional way, f_g towards the goal, f_{-g} away from the goal. It looks significant; it looks scientific; it is, in fact, bogus. If we could measure the forces *before* the child moves there might be something in it; as it is we cannot. The interpretation is all *ex post facto*: " there must have been a strong vector here, a weak one there," and so on. We are merely invited to use force terminology as a translation of perfectly adequate psychological terminology.

Again, suppose we want to get a child to do something which it does not want to do. We must hedge all alternative moves with negative vectors stronger than the negative vector which emanates from the task. Suppose we offer a reward, or conceive of freedom after the task is done as having positive values. There must be no way of reaching the reward save through the task. Shall the barrier between the child and the reward be conceived of as a simple bar, a line ? No, the child can get round it. What about a line curving round but not crossing itself and with a gap in it ? No, the child can get through the gap. It must be a line drawn round an area, no matter what shape, with no gap. This is the contribution of topology. Jourdan curves are mentioned.[1] I cannot but think it trivial.

There is something more to be said about the force analysis, this time in its favour. It does concentrate our minds on the actual situation, and that for many purposes is valuable. It is also useful when applied to group dynamics, as Lewin did in his *Frontiers of Group Dynamics*.[2] He takes the instance of racial discrimination in a town. It changes over a period of years or months. Forces making for discrimination are perhaps reduced, or forces against discrimination are increased—anyway, discrimination is, let us say, lessened. Or, of course, the reverse might happen. This is all expressed in formal symbolism, $f_g > f_s$, where the forces for discrimination are greater than the forces against. Again, since one has no means of measuring the forces, the symbolic apparatus really gives a false impression of scientific accuracy. However, a point is made. Many situations are as it were the resultant of opposing forces : they are, as Lewin

---

[1] *Topology*, by K. Lewin (McGraw-Hill, 1949).
[2] Tavistock Publications, 1952.

puts it, quasi-stationary equilibria, and it is often convenient to conceive of them in this way, thinking of social change in terms of a tipping of a balance one way rather than another. Again, the contribution here is more a matter of making a point than a transformation of social science into a mathematically calculable system of forces.

However, inspired by Lewin's notion of social interaction as a field of force, two interesting experiments have been performed. The first is the celebrated Lewin, Lippett, and White experiment with different styles of leadership.[1] Three groups of boys were subjected in turn to "autocratic," "democratic," and *laisser-faire* leadership. In the first the boys were told what to do, in the second they discussed with the leader what they were going to do, in the third they were left to their own devices. Various extra factors were introduced in each case, such as the absence of the leader and the visitation by a critical stranger. The general point, which is not indeed surprising, is that the boys comported themselves differently in the different fields. More significant is the measure of aggression in the case of authoritarian leadership as compared with democratic leadership. In the latter case there was a certain amount of aggression but not very much. In the former case there was either a good deal of aggression because, in Lewin's formulation, the collaborative forces which made against aggression were reduced, while repression increased the forces in favour of aggression; or there was apathy because the forces against aggression were positively supplemented by the forces of repression, so that the aggressive forces were effectively held in check. Held in check until a *laisser-faire* régime took the place of authoritarian and the pent-up aggression flared out. It must be noted that this experiment took place against an American cultural

[1] *J. of Soc. Psychol.*, Vol. 10 (1939), p. 271.

background, and that the results would not necessarily have been the same with children brought up under a different régime. At the same time it serves as one of the few examples of careful experimental procedure in the field of social science.

The second experiment concerns the feeding of babies on orange juice, and the changing of food habits of a group of American women during the Second World War. However, such topics are the stuff of everyday life and are only trivial if we think in terms of national crises and world movements. Also I must warn you that, as usual, the results were not startling. Two groups of mothers were brought together and one group was lectured on the virtues of orange juice; the other discussed the subject and collectively agreed to feed their babies on it. Which had the greater effect? Lecturing or collective commitment? Need I ask? The latter, of course. The same comparison was made with groups who were to be persuaded to change their own food habits, and with the same result. All this was done by Bavelas, a follower of Lewin, who found the same technique—mutual commitment—more efficacious in making changes in a factory than merely ordering people to do this or that. Discussion and mutual agreement or commitment have something of a consolidating effect on the individuals participating. In Lewin's phraseology a strong field of force is generated keeping each member of the group in line with the course of action agreed on. On these grounds we may say that wherever it is desirable to bring about a change in industry—increasing production, it may be—it is *groups* that have to be persuaded to change their *group* standards, rather than individuals.

Now it may be worth while to pass for a moment from the trivialities of orange juice to the portentous social changes that seem to be going on in modern China. There nearly every man and woman is a member of some group or another, and usually of more than one. A man at an office is a member of his office group or groups at various levels, so is a man or woman working in a factory, so are the staff and students in a university. They meet from time to time, clerks, departments, classes, or working teams, to discuss progress, to make suggestions, and to commit themselves. They meet, too, to discuss moral issues—as always in China, conduct is a matter of supreme concern. But this is not all. Every village has its peasant association, and every city is subdivided into small areas in which the resident families have their committees on education, women's affairs, housing, public security, and the like. The committees meet, the delegates from the families meet the families, and thus is formed a two-way channel of influence and criticism from the authorities to the households and from the households to the authorities. Everyone is implicated, and I think that there is no doubt that this mutual commitment is in part at any rate responsible for the great health drives, and the extraordinary campaign against illiteracy, which make a visit to a bookshop in Peking on a Sunday morning an unusual experience because one has to pick one's way through a throng of men, women, and children absorbed in their new achievement. Of course it may be said by some that all this group-commitment takes place in a nation-wide atmosphere of enthusiasm, in which the commitment of the group is in consonance with the aspiration of the people of China. This, I agree, makes a difference; but I feel sure that the face-to-face meetings as such play a very significant role in swaying the individual, confirming him in his intentions, and remoulding him if he shows signs of deviance.

The problem of mutual commitment is also relevant to the general issue of joint consultation in industry. This brings me to what I have called the therapeutic approach. I refer, of course, to the investigation into the consultative relationships in the Glacier Metal Company carried out by members of the Tavistock Institute of Human Relations.[1] It is impossible to describe the whole project in any detail. The very nature of the inquiry into the ramifications of executive control, administrative structure, and workers' representation on committees forbids it. The nature of the inquiry, however, is of interest and importance. Broadly speaking, under the influence of its enlightened managing director, the Company was aiming at an extension of consultative control, and the investigators proposed an inquiry into the stresses and strains that such a change would bring about. In a sense it is a change from a culture in which orders are given by an executive authority, which is responsible for the continued existence and healthy expansion of the factory in a competitive market, to a culture in which the responsibility is shared. In the opinion of the investigators, investigation is inseparable from therapy. They were there, not as mere observers, but as therapists. For this reason, and in order to ensure the confidence of all parties, they spent a considerable time getting themselves accepted by the Works Council and by other bodies as independent—not, that is to say, representing management or workers. They gave no advice, they only interpreted their patients—if one may call them so—to themselves and to one another. As they listened to the discussions at council meetings and watched the various policies and recommendations being handled from varying points of view, they noted the unconscious resistances displayed in the hesitation of speakers, the signs of irritation, and the attempts to avoid responsibility. They detected a sense of guilt and anxiety in the middle management range about giving orders, which confused their attitude towards the

[1] *The Changing Culture of a Factory,* by E. Jaques (Tavistock Publications, 1951).

consultative institution. They registered the predicament of the workers' representatives who had to commit their constituents. They sensed a kind of unanimous collusion between both parties to preserve the split between management and workers because of the emotional advantages it brought with it. The change of culture was particularly exhibited when the service departments changed over from piece rates to flat rates.[1] The Shop Council, which was responsible for departmental policy, had to discover whether the change had affected output. The measurement of output itself was difficult, but it was made the more so by the resistance of the workers. Under piece rates each worker feels himself responsible individually for the amount he does; it is up to him to earn what he can on the rate fixed for the job. When a flat-rate system was introduced, and its results had to be measured, the workers were called upon to consider the output of the department collectively, and this was in conflict with established norms. All these tensions in the Works Council, which had to reach unanimous decisions, and in the Shop Council of the Service Department, had to be brought to the surface, and—to use the favourite expression of the Tavistock Institute—" worked through."

Whether one agrees that scientific investigation, or scientific consultation, ought to be carried out in a therapeutic spirit, or whether one suspects some of the interpretations of over-subtlety, there can, I think, be no question of the value of the research. It brings to our notice subtle unconscious motivations which are undoubtedly operative in all human relations.

Much the same kind of situation where the play of unconscious factors upsets the smooth running of affairs

[1] " The Social and Psychological Impact of a Change in Method of Wage Payment," by E. Jaques, A. K. Rice, and J. M. M. Hill. *Human Relations*, Vol. IV, 1951, p. 315.

is to be found in the study made by C. M. Arensberg and D. Macgregor into the plight of the design engineers in what the investigators call the " Electric Equipment Company." [1] When the Company started manufacturing special measuring devices for the electrical industry, the design engineers were individually in touch with customers and dominated the production policy of the firm. The general ethos was that there should be no organization chart, that the competent man needs no supervision, and that technical expertise gave a man authority. As time went on and the Company expanded, a sales department took over customers and development and design committees on which the design engineers had but scant representation took over control of policy. The design engineers, who still stuck to their old cultural norms of independence and specialist control, were now faced with a changed and more formal culture, much more dominated by considerations of costing and marketing than had been the case in the good old informal " matey " days. No wonder they were accused of acting like *prime donne* by the rest of the organization, though they themselves were unaware of the causes of their dissatisfaction.

By way of introducing what I have called the analytic approach, I want to describe another factory group—the bank wirers of the Western Electric Company in America who figured in the well-known Hawthorne Experiment. The job was to wire banks of terminals for central office telephone equipment, of which there were two kinds— connector banks and selector banks. The nine wiremen worked in groups of three; one group sat in the front of the room, another in the middle—both engaged on connector work—and the third, engaged on selectors, at the

[1] " Determination of Morale in an Industrial Company," *Applied Anthropology*, Vol. I (1942), p. 12; cf. Homan's *The Human Group*, Chap. XIV (Kegan Paul, 1951).

back. Each group was attended by a solder-man, and there were two inspectors. The work was paid on a group piece-rate system, operating on a basic day-work rate which varied from person to person according to their output, efficiency, and skill. The selectors were paid at a lower rate than the connectors, and the solder-man at a lower rate than either. Thus a hierarchy of prestige, related to the front and back of the room, with all that that implies, was established. It was to the interests of all that as much work should be done as possible, but a rate of about 6,000 connectors a day was tacitly established, and deviations from this were met by the cry of " rate-buster " or " speed-king " if too much were done, and " chiseller " if too little. As time went on, an internal structure developed. The three bankmen in front, with their solder-man, formed the nucleus of a sub-group who talked and argued about high-class matters, and played games together in the break; while the lower-ranking men at the back formed another group who behaved less decorously and in general earned the disapproval of their superior colleagues. There was a great deal of detailed evidence of this, but at the same time there was a certain solidarity of the group as a whole, manifest in the fixed rate of output, and their joint feeling of belonging together *vis-à-vis* the other workers in the bank-wiring shop. All this is described in great detail by F. J. Roethlisberger and W. J. Dickson in their book *Management and the Worker* [1] and by several other writers who have directed their attention to the apparently inexhaustible source of information provided by the whole Hawthorne inquiry.

Now, one of the sociologists who have made use of the bank wirers and their culture is G. C. Homans. In a book called *The Human Group* he uses this study as a basis for his analytical treatment, and that is why I have

[1] Harvard Press, 1939.

mentioned it. He also makes use of Firth's study of the Tikopia, W. F. Whyte's account of the Norton Street Gang in Chicago, a study of a small town in disintegration called Hilltown, and the study of the "Electric Equipment Company" which I have already mentioned. Homans' analysis is of great interest, though I cannot here do justice to his contribution to the subject. In the first place he distinguishes between the external and internal systems of a group. This, I think, may be put like this: you have an environment—American culture in general and the Western Electric Company in particular, the material resources of a Polynesian island, Chicago in the depression, and the developing American scene with its improvements in transport, which formed the background of the disintegration of Hilltown. In these various contexts human beings meet for action and interaction. They join the Western Electric and have to do a job which demands a certain external system of organization; they have to make a livelihood, breed, look after their children, and perpetuate themselves on the island; they have to fill in their spare time in Chicago; or they have to make their living in New England. These requirements may be met in various ways, no doubt; but once a way has been found, a structure is established. Such a structure, however, generates interpersonal relationships—the internal system—which give rise to the elaborations of an internal culture: the bank wiremen develop their norms and laws; the Tikopian develop an elaborate family, lineage, and class system; the Norton Street gang develop the internal politics of prowess in the bowling alley; and the farmers of Hilltown develop their " bees " in the American sense of the word. Norms are established. As Malinowski put it: " Law and order arise out of the very processes which they govern," [1] a notion which I have already put before you.

[1] *The Human Group*, by G. C. Homans (Kegan Paul, 1951), p. 290.

Now, Homans, dealing with these diverse situations, attempts to formulate a set of hypotheses which are, as it were, applicable to them all. The three basic ones are: (1) " If the interactions between the members of a group are frequent in the external system, sentiments of liking will grow up between them, and these sentiments will lead in turn to further interaction, over and above the interaction of the external system." [1] The same thing has been said by Elton Mayo: " If a number of individuals work together to achieve a common purpose, a harmony of interests will develop among them to which individual self-interest will be subordinated." [2] (2) " When two persons interact with one another, the more frequently one of the two originates interaction for the other, the stronger will be the latter's sentiment of respect (or hostility) towards him, and the more nearly will the frequency of interaction be kept to the amount characteristic of the external system." [3] This is also turned round the other way to the effect that when A is of higher rank than B (as the connector wiremen were *vis-à-vis* the selectors), A will tend to initiate action in B more often that B does in A, which was indeed the case. Furthermore, to preserve authority and leadership, this interaction differential and the constraint it involves must be preserved. Some environments call for an " external system," in Homans' language, which is appropriate to the carrying out of complex activities. This means organization, and this, in turn, means a hierarchy. Within the system in Tikopia, where the father gives orders, the relationship between father and son is one of constraint; while the maternal uncle, whose function it is to give guidance and support, enters into a more interactive relationship, and the sentiment is one of

[1] op. cit., p. 112.
[2] *Political Problems of an Industrial Community* (Harvard Univ. Div. of Research, 1947), p. 21.
[3] *The Human Group*, p. 247.

affection; among the Trobriand Islanders, on the other hand, the reverse is the case: the father is the friend, the maternal uncle initiates action more than he has it initiated in him, and the relation is one of constraint. (3) " Persons who interact with one another frequently are more like one another in their activities than they are like other persons with whom they interact less frequently." Thus norms of action, as I have already said, grow out of the interactive situation; and where there is a difference in rank the person of high rank preserves his position, or even gets it (as in the case of the Norton Street Gang) by conforming to the norm better than anyone else. These norms may be strong or weak, according to the amount of interaction that they support. Accordingly we have a conception of a group in equilibrium. " A social system is in equilibrium and control is effective when the state of the elements that enter the system and of the mutual relationships between them is such that any small change in *one* of the elements will be followed by changes in the other elements tending to reduce the amount of that change." [1] Thus when external opportunity broke down the self-sufficient farm life of Hilltown so that the external system which met the old requirements of the environment was no longer required for the new ones, the interaction became less, the norms which were current in the old *internal* system broke down, *anomie* (as Durkheim called it) ensued, and conduct which would have brought reaction responses in the past now went unpunished.

I have not the space to deal fully with all Homans' hypotheses. I have chosen three (and elaborated them), which seem to me to be basic. These give us the following structural features : (*a*) A group as an interacting social system shaped to carry out a task set for it by the environment—which, as the examples show, may vary

[1] Homans, op. cit., p. 304.

from case to case. The group so shaped then sets up internal developments. (*b*) These internal developments are based on the rules of co-ordinate and super-ordinate interaction. (*c*) The aims of the group and the internal systematization precipitate norms which tend to constrain the individual, because he meets with unpleasantness somehow or another if he infringes them. Furthermore, these three features condition one another so that a change in the external system will be followed by a change in the internal system which will involve a change in the norms.

The spontaneity of the establishment of this kind of structure may be illustrated by an experiment carried out by Sherif.[1] He took twenty-four boys camping. On the basis of a sociometric assessment he *separated* friends from one another into two groups. These groups—the " Bulldogs " and the " Red Devils " as they called themselves—had the chance of carrying out their own camping activities, building bivouacs, going on expeditions, and so on. Very soon a leadership hierarchy developed in response to the requirement for organization; the boys in the groups became more closely allied to one another than to their old friends and a system of law and loyalty developed. This was heightened when competitions between the two groups were organized, and still more intensified when the experimenter so arranged things as to make one group believe that the other had behaved in an underhand fashion. *Then*, hostility was aroused, with its concomitant features of stereotyping and cartooning.

It seems to me that with Homans' hypotheses we have the theoretical basis for the study of small groups which corresponds to—and would, if satisfactory, form part of —the required theoretical structure I mentioned earlier.

[1] *Social Psychology at the Crossroads*, ed. by J. H. Rohrer and M. Sherif (1952, Free Press), p. 388.

Two final points may be made. First, I think that the stress laid on action is important. One of the reasons why the groups flourish in China is, I feel sure, that action is so obviously demanded. There is obvious need to clean the streets, to increase output, to abolish illiteracy, and so on, just as in the last war there was obvious need for civil defence. With us there are no such obvious and obviously attainable needs. This is not the whole story, of course, but it is important. The need for increased output is conveyed by the newspapers and not by the spectacle of everyday life concretely before us. The lesson—or rather the hypothesis —is that if we want to create groups, or encourage group life, over and above such groupings as the external systems inevitably provide in factory, office, and service life, then we must develop them on the basis of action: we must, in fact, give them something to do.

But, to turn to the second point, do we need groups and group affiliation over and above what is structurally inevitable? This is so great an issue, involving topics like the nature and needs of human beings, that it is almost foolhardy to introduce it at this juncture. A word, however, must be said. "Membership of a group," says Homans,[1] "sustains a man, enables him to maintain his equilibrium under the ordinary shocks of life, and helps him to bring up children who will in turn be happy and resilient." Accordingly if a civilization is to maintain itself, it "must preserve at least a few of the characteristics of a group, though necessarily on a much more expanded scale."[2] And it may be argued that such cannot be if you have an economy which involves divided and opposed interests. The celebrated " contradiction " may be translated to the social-psychological sphere.

[1] *The Human Group*, p. 457.
[2] ibid., p. 456.

Now, no one will deny the ill effects of a sense of isolation or rejection. Nor can one deny the exhilaration of co-operative participation. And yet many people seem to " maintain their equilibrium under the ordinary shocks of life " with the aid of comparatively few congenial friends; not everyone seems to relish group participation. Many prefer privacy. Mr Paul Halmos [1] says that this cult of privacy is to be deplored; Fromm,[2] if I understand him rightly, says, on the other hand, that our fear of freedom is neurotic. I do not know the answer to all this. I confess that I should like to see the study of small groups and the establishment of the rules of harmony and equilibrium within them supplemented by a study of healthy non-groupers, if any such may be found, so as to discover under what conditions of infantile treatment, home environment, and subsequent experience it is possible to fashion a way of life which is satisfying, but which does not require the sustaining encouragement of group membership. Of course I recognize that my interest in this question is extremely unfashionable, and that no such research is likely to be initiated (let alone financed) unless I do it myself.

[1] *Solitude and Privacy* (Kegan Paul, 1951).
[2] *Fear of Freedom* (Kegan Paul, 1942).

CHAPTER V

Assimilation

IN this and the next chapter I want to take two fields of research in order to illustrate the complexity of factors which have to be taken into consideration in social science, and therefore the variety of research methods which are employed. These are: assimilation and deviance. The first because it seems to me to bring out the variety contained in a relatively narrow field of inquiry, the second because I think that a good deal of discussion on the matter centres round the immediate highly-emotionally-toned situation and that more general considerations are therefore liable to be missed. In both these fields the formal situational aspects of society (demographic, ecologic, and economic), face-to-face interaction, the structural aspect, and the belief and value climate are relevant. In both of them problems of analysis, methodology, description, fact-finding, psychological interpretation, and theoretical contributions are to be found.

The general topic of assimilation is obvious enough. It could, of course, be expanded to include the socialization of children into any community in which they are born. It usually refers to " the process through which an immigrant or alien loses the modes of behaviour previously acquired in another society and gradually takes on the ways of the new society "—or at any rate something like that. The problem of definition will occupy us later. I indicated that the field of inquiry was a relatively narrow one, and by that I meant that our attention is focused upon a fairly precise problem. The range of examples covers pretty well the whole of human history. Processes of assimilation went on throughout the histories of China, of Egypt, of Greece, of Rome, and of our own country—wherever, in fact, aliens were absorbed. It is, as usual, only in comparatively recent years that the subject has become one for systematic investigations, and for obvious reasons the " melting-pot " of America has provided the scene of the great bulk of these inquiries.

The American scene, however, does not suit my immediate purpose so well as a smaller one. The story in America is too long and too complicated. Immigration in the early days was quite different from immigration when the frontier was closed. " Plantation immigration " is quite different from immigration in small numbers into cities, and so on. As an illustration of general principles America is too complex. I am going to use, instead, the researches carried out by Dr Eisenstadt into the problems of assimilation in the State of Israel.

Clearly the first approach to the subject must be via formal demographic information. From this we learn that the estimated Jewish population of Israel was about 24,000 in 1882, nearly 84,000 in 1922, and about 909,000 in June 1949. This enormous increase is accounted for by the arrival of thousands of immigrants every year, particularly in 1924–25 when the rate was 285 per thousand of the population, in 1935 when the high rate of 192 per thousand of the population was reached, and during 1948–49 when the rate for the first six months of 1949 was 170 per thousand of the population.

Most of them came from the USSR, Poland, Austria and Germany, the Balkans, Yemen, Irak, Iran, Turkey, North Africa, and a few from other countries. The quota supplied from each country varied from year to year, and I will not trouble you with any more figures of this rather arid kind. It is clear enough that if one is going to study the assimilation of immigrants one wants to know the number who arrive and the size of the receiving population. There are, indeed, other things one wants to know, and this is a good example of the way in which the material provided by the official sources of statistics is influenced by sociological research. This matter will crop up again, but two instances may be mentioned here. If it is agreed that the young are more easily assimilated than the old—and research often bears out the expectation of common sense—then it is important that the ages of immigrants should be registered. Again, if Dr Eisenstadt's views about the significance of the family—which we shall come to in a moment—are valid, then it is important to know whether whole families immigrate together or only single persons.

The bare formal statistics, however, important though they are, merely set the stage. The drama of social interaction has yet to begin. The population of Israel can be divided into three strata: the original inhabitants before the great immigration, to whom we must add such so-called " Oriental Jews " as came later; the " pioneers " ; and the more recent influx.[1] Leaving aside the " Oriental Jews " for the moment, the " pioneers " who founded the State of Israel came from a variety of nations, imbued with the desire to found a new society. They came from Jewish communities which had been in close touch with the enlightenment; they had been influenced by western capitalist development; they felt that traditional Jewish cultures could not exist under the conditions of modern society. They were not inspired by the economic motive, which inspired so much emigration, but rather by the aim of establishing a Jewish nation, which meant that they were prepared to work in fields and factories

---

[1] " The Sociological Structure of the Jewish Community in Palestine," by S. N. Eisenstadt. *Jewish Social Studies*, Vol. X, 1948, p. 4.

so as to contribute to the establishment of a viable social order.   Status was bound up with service, and the great co-operative enterprises were established.

As time went on the Jewish State was established with its bureaucratic apparatus and it was to this that later immigrants had to adapt themselves.   It was a world in which the material symbols of status were the reward for hard work in the social cause, they were the insignia of roles, the achievement of which was the reward of a long period of apprenticeship.   The new-comers were not inspired by the same pioneer spirit.   " For these people," says Dr Eisenstadt, " immigration to Palestine did not differ essentially from the ordinary process of immigration." [1]   Assimilation was made difficult by (1) " the tempo of the immigration and the decreasing ratio of the existing population to new-comers; (2) the difficult post-war economic situation; and (3) the growing bureaucratization of the social structure of the new State and the concomitant widening of social distance and the rise of status-anxiety." [2]

Several investigations were undertaken by the Israel Institute for Research in Public Opinion and by the Hebrew University at Jerusalem.   Dr Weinberg investigated the attitude of some 357 immigrants from Holland, and Dr Foa studied the assimilation of Yemenite Jews. [3]

A more detailed survey was carried out by Dr Eisenstadt in 1949 on some 1,000 families who had arrived in Israel since 1948.   Dr Weinberg and the Institute for Research in Public Opinion found that it takes about ten years for a new immigrant to be fully integrated, and Dr Eisenstadt's samples had been there on an average

[1] " The Sociological Structure of the Jewish Community in Palestine," by S. N. Eisenstadt.   *Jewish Social Studies*, Vol. X, 1948, p. 5.
[2] " The Social Development of Israel," *Middle Eastern Affairs*, Vol. II, 1951, p. 166.
[3] Bachi: " Statistical Research on Immigrants in the State of Israel." Cultural Assimilation of Immigrants.   *Population Studies Supplement*, March 1950, p. 55.

only nineteen months, but, whatever may happen to them eventually, he was able to detect certain factors of importance which would aid or impede assimilation. His immigrants came from Yemen, Turkey, North Africa, Bulgaria, Yugoslavia, and Eastern and Central Europe. His first task was to consider criteria of assimilation, and he defines these as: (1) the extent of stable social relations with the old inhabitants; (2) the extent of social segregation of immigrants, either voluntary or enforced; (3) the extent of successful performance of roles inherent in the different spheres of the new social structure; (4) the extent of deviant behaviour; and (5) the extent of personal and group aggression, specifically aggression towards the new social structure and its symbols.[1] He also compiled indices of predisposition to accept the changed conditions which confronted them, and he found—as we might expect—that a predisposition to change was a fundamental factor in assimilation; furthermore, he found it more prevalent among the age group fifteen to twenty-two than among those who were older. Far more interesting for our purpose is that this readiness to accept change differed according to country of origin, and according to the solidarity of the immigrant's family life. Furthermore, these were related.

The families were divided into three types: (1) the "traditional sector"—Yemenite Jews and some from North Africa who had experienced a certain amount of social autonomy with considerable devotion to Jewish tradition; (2) the "transitional sector"—Central and Eastern Europe and also North Africa who had experienced very little autonomy and strong aspirations towards entrance into Gentile society, which was blocked by the fact of their being Jews (this gave rise to what Eisenstadt calls: "status-anxiety"); (3) the "secure sector"—

[1] "Absorption of Immigrants in Israel" (Jewish Agency for Palestine, 1951), p. 8.

from Yugoslavia and Bulgaria, where they had been an accepted section of the community, so that being a Jew was a source of a strong feeling of security. There were also immigrants from DP camps who were classified among the second and third groups. Now, of the traditional sector the majority (248 to 84) were predisposed to change, and so were the majority of the " secure " sector (189 to 12). The middle sector were the reverse, 35 were predisposed to change, against 379 who were not.

The solidarity of family life was also found to be correlated with predisposition to change, the explanation being that change requires a capacity to stand on one's own feet, to endure hardship in preparation for happier days, and that the solidary family provides one with a secure basis for such an enterprise. And, we need not be surprised that the solidary family was found more often in the traditional and the secure sections than in the sections plagued with status-anxiety, because in the latter case either being a member of a Jewish family is a felt disgrace or else one is looked upon as an instrument for improving the family position, or both.

They arrived, then, with various histories and attitudes behind them, not aiming at founding or improving a new society, but rather looking for social and economic security.

The land of promise did not flow with milk and honey. They had bureaucrats to deal with and the opportunities offered were meagre. It therefore mattered that the agencies who received them should plan an ordered existence for them and not break, or appear to break, their promises; it mattered that the bureaucrats should take a special personal interest in them, and it mattered that they should be able to penetrate into the groups and organizations of the old inhabitants, or at least make some effective contact with them.

And how did they fare ? Dr Eisenstadt distinguishes

five types of adaptation. (1) The isolate apathetic family, coming mainly from the sector with high status-anxiety. They participate but little, they feel frustrated in their hopes and blame " the system " for their ills, and family life collapses. (2) The isolated stable family. They keep themselves rather to themselves in family unity, critical of the bureaucracy but identifying themselves with the new State, and yet not taking any determined step to participate in it. (3) The isolated active family. These cut themselves off from co-immigrants, but participate in civic organizations and play their part, so far as they can, in the new society. They are mostly made up of " ex-*élite* families from Central and Eastern Europe," with strong feelings of identification with the new State, but a good deal of criticism of the bureaucratization that they have found there, and of the reserve of the old inhabitants. (4) The cohesive ethnic group. These families preserve close contact with one another, and preserve the traditional forms of life. They are anxious to participate in the new order, but largely by way of imposing their own more traditionally religious ideas upon it. Accordingly they criticize the lack of religiosity among the people who hold the dominant positions in the régime. Being organized into ethnic groups they have their own *élite*, and their adaptation is related to the circulation of the *élite* within them. If the young, who, as we have seen, are likely to appreciate the new situation better than the old, are given their chance, the participation becomes more extensive; if this is not the case, then internal disruption occurs in the family life which may display itself in deviant conduct. It is notable that in this type when assimilation is baulked because of incompatibility between the immigrants and the receiving cultures, the response takes the form of collective movements against the central values of the social system, and not mere isolated "regressive"

reactions.   Finally we have (5) the self-transforming
cohesive ethnic group, almost all of whom come from
Yugoslavia and Bulgaria, who are prepared to alter
their way of life, while at the same time preserving their
unity. They preserve a group-identification directed
towards support of the new order.   In so far as they are
not successful, their reaction is organized in political
terms, compatible with the new institutional structure,
thereby making possible a political split between their
élite and those of the receiving country. The significance of the *élite* in the last two types of cohesive ethnic
groups is clear: they are the mediators between the incoming group and the existing authorities, and they
occupy, therefore, a key position in the assimilation
process.

Before commenting on this it will be convenient to
glance at the problem of the " Oriental Jews " [1] who have
already been mentioned. They consist of Jews who
were in Palestine before the great immigration, and of
Jews who came from the Arab countries. They were
untouched by western capitalism and its attendant
enlightenments and social movements. They therefore
aspired to preserve all the traditional features of Judaism,
and came to Palestine inspired by Messianic enthusiasm.
Their traditional occupations were small handicraft,
peddling, small-scale trades, and unskilled labour, and—
for the *élite*—banking and large-scale trade. The *élite*
was one of wealth and traditional learning. They arrived
in Palestine hoping to carry on in the old way, unham-
pered by persecution; they found a very different state
of affairs. The *élite* were able to make some sort of
terms with the new society; they could get rich and make
new contacts or they could establish themselves in the
new secularized professions. This meant a break with

[1] " The Oriental Jews in Israel," by S. N. Eisenstadt. *Jewish Social
Studies*, Vol. XII, 1950, p. 199.

the old traditions and left their followers without guidance. The followers, on the other hand, found that the occupations they were expected by their families to pursue were not viable in the new economy. There was a discontinuity between the traditional home life and the life in the world outside—a situation of what Durkheim called "anomie," or unintegratedness. Therefore, on the hypothesis that individual conduct is guided into socially acceptable channels by the presence of a socially recognized system of rules, we are not surprised that a number of the second-generation Orientals lapsed into delinquency, frequently changed their jobs, and aimed at getting possession of the material signs of status—smart clothes and the like—as soon as possible and without passing through the recognized stages of apprenticeship. This latter point was revealed by a study of family budgets —a good example of the use to which such a field of inquiry can be put. One group, however, were less prone to this disorganization: the Kurdish families. These were mainly unskilled workers who were prepared to advance slowly and had a " positive attitude towards work and a positive attitude towards acquiring skills, which were congenial to their new situation." Their aspirations fitted their opportunities.

This somewhat detailed account of assimilation in Israel brings out the following points: (1) the interweaving of data from all four aspects of social science: formal statistics, social structure, beliefs and values, and the more intimate field of actual social action; (2) it throws some light on the significance of the concept of harmony, integration, and coherence in a society as a factor responsible for harmony, integration, and coherence in the individual; and (3) more particularly it brings out significant factors which have to be taken into consideration when dealing with the problem of assimilation in general.

It is clear that assimilation is a complex process depending on (*a*) the attitude and aspirations of the immigrant; (*b*) the attitude of the receiving community; (*c*) the opportunities offered to the immigrant to satisfy his aspirations and to mix with the society into which he has come; and (*d*) the degree to which the immigrant has a sense of security derived either from his own people or from the receiving society. It is clear also that the immigrants respond to the situation in different ways, and that one way is to cling together if there are significant numbers of them. Lastly, it is clear that the situation in Israel is in many ways peculiar. There are certain common elements—their common religion, and common plight among the Gentiles—which give the situation there a peculiar flavour, though one which by no means ensures an absence of bitterness, as we have seen. This very peculiarity of the Jewish problem was one of the reasons for choosing it; it calls attention to the fact that the problem of assimilation is bound to vary from one context to another.

Besides the Jewish context Dr Eisenstadt distinguishes four other types of immigration.[1] First, agricultural immigrants in Europe, such as Polish and Italian peasants settling in France. In their case their motive was economic, but their orientation was towards their homeland, and in the preservation of their traditions and distinctive way of life they were supported by the *élite* of priests and teachers who came with them. While they were merely farming, their particularistic role values were compatible with the society about them, but difficulties arose when the universalistic demands of the modern State came their way, when, for instance, they were expected to do military service, or when, in pursuit of better jobs, they went into urban areas. The need for the consoling influence of friends about them was

[1] *Absorption of Immigrants* (Kegan Paul, 1954).

revealed by an inquiry in 1928 [1] into the high rate of delinquency and mental pathology among Poles (double the rate among Frenchmen of the same age). It was found that in nearly all the cases examined the subjects were agricultural labourers who had been sent to work individually on isolated farms, where no one knew their language or understood their situation. They could not stand it. When a rule was made for the districts in which the inquiry was held that no Poles should be sent to work by themselves, the proportion of delinquents and mentally deranged fell by 60 per cent, though elsewhere it remained the same.

The second type Dr Eisenstadt calls: the " planta-tion pattern," illustrated by immigrants in Brazil. Here again, the Germans retained, and were encouraged to retain, a loyalty to their homeland, as is illustrated by the persistent preference for speaking German, even when they moved into more populous districts. Surveys have been made in Brazil into the persistence of the mother tongue in successive generations as an index of assimila-tion, and it was found that different immigrants from different countries of origin vary remarkably in the extent to which they are prepared to change in this respect. This is doubtless partly due to linguistic affinities, but it cannot be entirely explained in this way.[2] The " plantation " context differs from the previous one in that the planta-tion is definitely run on commercial lines, that is to say the old traditional subsistence features which attach to farming are absent. This means that the motif of achievement is there from the start, and many immigrants are affected by it and aspire to enter the competitive world. This, in turn, is liable to cause resentment on

---

[1] " The Assimilation of Foreigners in France," by G. Mauco in *Cultural Assimilation of Immigrants*, p. 19. (Supplement to Population Studies, 1950.)

[2] " Immigration to Brazil," by Gingio Mortara, in *Cultural Assimilation of Immigrants*, p. 40.

the part of the old inhabitants. In Hawaii, however, where a plantation structure was established, the Chinese who came merely to make some money and then go home found, as the economy expanded, that there was plenty of room for them. The result was that they gradually penetrated into proprietary, clerical, and professional occupations, and distributed themselves throughout the community, changing their loyalty to the community of adoption.[1]

A third and quite different context is the Asiatic colonial pattern, which has its parallels in parts of South Africa. Here you have groups of traders filling a gap between the colonial group and the indigent group. They live their own lives and preserve their own traditions, and all may be well so long as the colonial pattern is preserved. When, however, active indigenous movements for independence develop, a struggle for power is likely to ensue.

Finally comes America with its " pluralistic " substructure of ethnic groups. Here again the attitude of the immigrants is important. Some came to find freedom of religious worship and some to make their fortunes. It is true, of course, that the latter far outnumber the former. They tend to group themselves in ethnic areas, originally, no doubt, of their own free will, but also partly because only certain districts are available for occupation. Ease of assimilation also depends, as we have seen, on the compatibility of their own culture with that of America. Warner and Srole [2] have made a ranking order of assimilability from this point of view. It is most easy for English-speaking Protestants; next come, in descending order: Protestants who do not speak English, English-speaking Catholics and other non-

[1] " The Relation between Position and Status in the Assimilation of Chinese in Hawaii," by Claus Glick. *Am. J. of Sociol.* (1942), p. 667, and *Sociological Analysis*, by Wilson and Kolb, p. 704.

[2] *Social Systems of American Ethnic Groups* (Yale Univ. Press, 1945).

Protestants, non-Protestants who speak allied Indo-European languages, English-speaking non-Christians, and last of all, non-Christians who do not speak English.[1]

Another factor is the availability of occupations and the way in which these fit with the skills or lack of skills possessed by the immigrants. The farmers found land; the Jews from eastern Europe, trained in clothing and shoe production, were able to establish themselves; but Italians, Greeks, and Poles who came from an agrarian background found it difficult to fit into the industrial culture for which they supplied unskilled labour. The effect of this on the Poles has been the subject matter of a classic of sociological literature: Thomas and Znaniecki's *The Polish Peasant in Europe and America*.[2]

The "pluralistic" solution, as one might call it—the ecological grouping of immigrants—has complex effects. On the one hand it affords some protection to the newcomer, and that, as we have seen, is important. It also provides a basis for organization and the setting up of formal agencies which help their members. On the other hand it tends to perpetuate the old culture, and this provides what one might call a reaction basis for the younger generation who are desperately anxious to fit into the American way of life, often find it difficult to establish themselves, and who blame their origins. This, again, may lead to family disunion, and, when the old norms are rejected and new ones only superficially accepted, to delinquency and mental disturbance. One may also say that when immigrants have been unable to fit into positions and roles already established, they have then established and, as it were, institutionalized deviant positions and roles for themselves.

This rapid glance at some of the situations has only covered cases where the incoming group is ethnically

---

[1] *Society*, by MacIver and Page, p. 129.
[2] Badger, 1918.

different from the receiving society. The vast immigration of Germans from the East to the West, some of them moved in accordance with the Control Plan for Transfer of Population, and most of them refugees, making a total of eight million persons to be absorbed, differs from the other cases. In a way it is more like the case of Israel because the immigrants have traditions similar to those of the receiving community. The difficulty is that, owing to the uneven distribution among the Länder, there is very little room for them. They are, many of them, destitute, but they have the same legal status as the rest of the population. Many of them hope and expect to return, and are encouraged in this belief by their leaders, which means that they tend to resist assimilation and develop their own organizations, which aim at political influence. This, like the organizations among the recent immigrants in Israel, is having its effect on the political structure of western Germany. The inhabitants are hostile to the immigrants, especially in Bavaria, while the immigrants resent their inferior economic and social position and feel that there should be some equality of sacrifice.

Now, all the types of immigration which I have mentioned have only one thing in common: the arrival of people, singly or in groups, who intend to take up residence in an established population permanently or temporarily. The concept of assimilation itself has become blurred. The definition with which we started ran: " The process through which an immigrant loses the modes of behaviour previously acquired in another society and gradually takes on the ways of the new society." Such a definition hardly applies to the German situation, where the cultural characteristics of the immigrant Germans are very like those of their hosts. It hardly applies to the peasant type or to the plantation type or to the Asiatic-colonial type. It seems to me that we ought to think rather in terms of a scale of accommodation ranging from relatively segregated groupings at one end to complete absorption at the other. Successful accommodation will be measured in terms of: (1) the attitude of the receiving population to the immigrants; (2) the attitude of the immigrants to their position, and their conduct in it; and (3) such indices as are relevant to the kind of accommodation at which the immigrants are aiming. This means that such well-known indices as intermarriage and language may not be universally applicable. It means also that the prognostication of success will require different data from case to case. Such generalizations as one can make, save in so far as one registers certain factors as universally relevant, are bound to be of limited application. We can, however, say that age, sex, religion, skill, education, whether the immigrants come singly or in families, and the reasons why they have migrated, are likely to be significant. The peculiar fact is that such information is not always available. The sources of official information are: census returns and immigration returns, and in these there is often a confusion even about the country of origin. In the interests of providing more information the United Nations Population Committee have attempted to formulate standard tabulations of information to be used by all countries.[1] This is another instance of the effect of social research on statistical registration.

It will be noticed that I have not mentioned one group whose accommodation has proved a matter of special concern: the coloured ethnic group residing among a predominantly white population. They present special difficulties because of their conspicuousness, and because of the prejudices against them on the part of many

[1] " Statistics for Studying the Cultural Assimilation of Migrants," by Max Lacioux and Edith Adams. *Cultural Assimilation of Immigrants*, p. 69.

receiving societies. These two factors, and especially the first, are of course of very great importance, and the accommodation of a coloured group, which aspires to carry out a wide range of roles which are normally allocated to members of the white population, is certainly a special case, partly because of the ease with which the white population can display their resentment by refusing access to public conveyances, hotels, restaurants, and so on. Granted this, the general problem is, I think, no different in principle from that of accommodating any group of immigrants. The attitudes of the receiving population, the aspirations of the new-comers and the opportunities offered by the social structure are relevant in all cases of immigration; the case of coloured people is special only because the attitude of the receiving population is so often hostile. This means that to improve accommodation it is the receiving population who have to be re-educated in their case, whereas in most other cases it is rather the immigrant who must be persuaded to change his ways.

So far as this country is concerned we learn from the *Preliminary Report on the 1951 Census* that, for the first time in the past century, there has been a net gain of some 745,000 under the heading of civilian migration during the twenty years from 1931 to 1951. This, of course, comes as no surprise, save perhaps that we may be impressed by the size of the figure. It is estimated that " about two-thirds of the total occurred prior to the war with an average gain of about 66 thousands per annum over the years 1931 to 1939, after which it diminished during the six war years with an average annual gain of about 48 thousands, after which it was converted to a loss on balance during the immediate period of post-war resettlement and has since been followed by less signifi-cant and less consistent changes in the more recent years."
It is important to recognize that the figure of 745,000 is a

net figure—the balance of immigration over emigration, and that emigration would appear to include the posting of armed forces overseas. Furthermore, of course, it does not only consist of persons from foreign countries.

Now, when one tries to find out how many people have come to this country as refugees or under the European Voluntary Worker scheme, or by any other avenue, one comes up against serious difficulties. Presumably the census returns, when published, will give us precise information; meanwhile one has to rely on Home Office releases and information from the International Refugee Organization. However, in July 1950 it was announced in Parliament that there were some 425,578 aliens in the United Kingdom. Of these, 86,346 were settled in the United Kingdom by the International Refugee Organization. The largest group of aliens are Poles for whom the figure given in 1950 was 145,756. In addition there are some 46,000 Ukrainians, 46,697 Germans, and over 20,000 from the Baltic countries. Besides these there are Czechs, Hungarians, and Yugoslavs.

They have come here in various ways: many of the Poles were in the armed forces and preferred to remain in the United Kingdom; about 80,000 came under the European Voluntary Worker Scheme; about 6,000 came under the "Distressed Relatives Scheme," [1] 30,000 were dependants of members of Polish forces, and others under a limited scheme of sponsorship from camps in Germany and Austria.

Since 1946, 34,000 pre-war refugees have been naturalized, and 3,500 Poles have been naturalized between 1950 and 1951.

Some of them live in hostels, either under the charge of the National Assistance Board, or under the Ministry of

[1] Statistics of Foreigners Entering and Leaving the United Kingdom, HMSO, Cmd. 3967, p. 4.

Labour, or supplied by employers; while a greater number live in private accommodation.

In general their difficulties seem to be concerned with security of employment, housing, and a general feeling of not being wanted—at least, this last was given by refugees in Bradford as grounds for their not entering into the social activities open to them. The Trade Unions feel that they have to safeguard the interests of their own countrymen, and local authorities are inclined to give priority in housing to English applicants rather than to foreigners. The refugees have also, on occasion, felt ill used because they thought they could change their jobs after one year, and it turned out that they had to wait three. In addition to all this, it is said in one report that " psychologically England is probably the most difficult of all countries in which to be a refugee." We are so very odd.

All these facts have emerged from such research as I have been able to come across.[1] There is, however, a very interesting field of inquiry lying ready for the social scientist if he can get the facilities to carry it out. From what I have heard—and this must be regarded as mere gossip—it seems that readiness to settle down depends in this country, as elsewhere, on such factors as: the extent to which available employment matches the skill and education of the employee; closely bound up with this: the social status of the refugee in his land of origin; and—perhaps most important of all—the degree to which the refugee thinks he will never return. Apparently many refugees from Baltic countries will say : " We don't want to be assimilated "; they are awaiting " liberation." Again the *élite* are important here as they are elsewhere. It is said that the Poles are hindered in their settling down by a section of them who insist that

[1] An account of assimilation of Poles is given in " Poles in England," by T. Zubrzycki (PhD Thesis. Univ. of London, 1953).

they must preserve their national distinctiveness. The Ukrainians, too, have their own newspaper and publishing department, their own Catholic and Greek churches.

The individual refugee, living apart from his fellow nationals, may present a problem of interest to the psychologist who might wish to study his processes of adaptation. The groups of refugees who live in hostels or who form communities in cities provide, it seems to me, a kind of experimental situation for the student of small groups. Interaction no doubt keeps them together, but what defences, if any, do they put up against the absorption of the group into the wider society? On the other hand we might ask: by what means—if we want to avoid "pluralism"—can such groups be broken down? Again, we can study at first hand the problem of the second-generation immigrant: Will he wish to become more English than the English, and if not, why not? Finally there is the problem of culture contact: Are there cultural differences between the various groups of immigrants which hinder accommodation to varying extents?

I mention such questions because I think that the study of the problem of assimilation is not only of topical interest, not only of immediate practical interest, but of theoretical interest as well.

CHAPTER VI

Deviance

THE concept of deviance implies the concept of order. We have at the back of our minds the notion of a social system with its normative regulations, and deviance is the departure on the part of participants from culturally expected rules of conduct. This abstract pattern is a kind of ideal type in many of the senses of that expression. It is, in fact, never realized. In simple small-scale societies, as Malinowski and my predecessor Professor Firth in his Josiah Mason Lectures on Social Organization have pointed out, the cultural pattern is abstracted by the social anthropologists from the uneven personal conduct of the actors who weave it. We have an abstract notion of the dance, but in the actual dancing each dancer has his or her own style, and the young lady in the back row may want to attract special attention to herself. Although each member of a society becomes a separate human being, recognizing himself as different from the rest through social intercourse, although he acquires the ambitions, specific desires, and resentments that he does acquire through contact with other people, he does absorb his experience in his own way. He himself has his own specific endowment of potentialities, and he has his own unique version of the culture which has produced him.

I have put the matter in this rather cumbersome way because I want to avoid language which implies that members of societies have certain ambitions, desires, and aims by nature—by the mere fact of their being human

beings.   There are, no doubt, certain needs which must
be satisfied if they are to survive at all, but I see no
reason to suppose that there is a *natural* urge to be
ambitious, warlike, ritualistic, self-seeking, self-sacrific-
ing, or whatever may be the cultural values which any
given person is brought up to revere.   He will, of
course, when he reaches awareness of himself, be concerned about himself and about the regard others have
for him; he will be drawn well into the social pattern, or
only partly so, according to his experience of satisfaction
or the reverse.   But whether that means that he will be a
good hunter or find himself shamed by his ineptitude, a
good fighter or shamed by his cowardice, an effective
competitor in the race for money or a failure, a devoted
servant of society or a guilty self-seeker, will depend not
only on his initial endowment (a residual category at the
best), but also on the standards held up to him by the
cultural representatives and by the actual personal
treatment he receives in childhood and in later life.

We might imagine a simple agricultural community
in which the children are slowly infiltrated into the social
order, having recognized duties appropriate to their
capacities at different periods of their lives.   The
standards might be simple, the fulfilment of them rewarding, and the goals adjusted to the aspirations aroused.
It is true that conflict cannot be avoided.   The desire to
eat an apple, which is culturally reputable at certain times
and places, may be present at the wrong moment.   Theft
might occur.   And other conflicts between desire and
the rules can be envisaged; but the demands of the
society and the rewards available might be such as to
reduce such conflicts, and therefore deviance, to a minimum.

Again, one can imagine a highly ritualistic society
such, according to Mead and Bateson, as the Balinese.
Their conduct is intimately guided by detailed rules, and

safety lies in keeping them. In this case there is an inherent danger. Provided the situations are always such as to prompt the correct behaviour, all is well, assuming the rules to have been adequately acquired; but when a novel situation presents itself, panic may be the result.

Again, there are societies such as my first example, in which there is continuity of learning—in which, that is to say, a boy or girl grows gradually into adulthood, learning a little more as he or she grows older. But there are also societies in which there is a discontinuity, in which a life of irresponsibility suddenly gives place to a life of responsibility. Such is the case with the Manus, as described by Margaret Mead. Such, too, is the case with our own urban society, where boys and girls have to leave their homes in order to acquire skills quite different from the ones which they have learnt from their parents. Most of them are suddenly plunged into the outside world, in which they have the ambiguous status of being neither adults nor children.

Finally, in our own large-scale competitive society we do not have a set of simple rules, agreed to by all, with what one might call uniform danger points. We do not have a society in which the interests of all members are congruent. We have a society in which many interests conflict, and a society in which there are many different standards of conduct. The significance of this will, I hope, appear later on.

My purpose in mentioning these examples is to point out that different societies put different pressures upon their members, and therefore every society provides its own deviancy hazards. This is, I think, part of what Durkheim meant when he said: *Chaque état de civilization a sa criminalité propre.*[1] But he meant more than that. A simple society in which the members all performed their roles adequately and with satisfaction would be static.

[1] *Régles de la Méthode Sociologique,* 1947 ed., p. 75.

Change could come only from without, or by the pressures of increasing numbers on the means of subsistence and on the demands of organization. The presence of the deviant, who does not accept the roles offered to him, is a prerequisite for social change from within. We have to think of a society as an ever-changing continuum, producing its characteristic quota of deviants at any given moment, and, having produced them, being by so much changed, and in its new state producing deviants characteristic of it, and so on.

The sociological approach has, I think, been neglected; it is true that we learn from Walter C. Reckless [1] that crime is rare among such groups as a number of American Indians, former Chinese communities, modern European village communities including Swiss municipalities, the Danish parish, German villages, and Irish rural areas. The determining difference, we are told, is " a sociological factor of stability," which does not, after all, tell us very much. We know, too, that different communities forbid different things; but that, again, does not carry us very far. What we are most used to, apart from the official registration of deviance, is the personal approach.

This does not, of course, mean that sociological factors are left entirely out of account. We have discussions about the influence of the films, the significance of economic and political crises, the part played by poverty, and the diverse opportunities provided by rural as distinct from urban life. Such factors are shown to be significant in the ætiology of deviance by the presentation of statistical evidence. We agree, or disagree, as the case may be, with the calculations, and then we say: " There are many who are poor but honest, there are many who survive crises unscathed, there are many who live in cities and yet emerge from Woolworth's

[1] *Criminal Behaviour* (N.Y., 1940), p. 26.

unembarrassed by illicitly obtained articles; and thousands of children go to gangster films without re-enacting the story in everyday life." The answer is that such influences affect only those whose " thresholds " of delinquency are low. The greater the pressure the higher must be the threshold to resist it. The assumption is that everyone is brought up to be law abiding, but that the incidence of crises, poverty, temptation, and so on makes the keeping of the rules more difficult to some than to others. In each case, therefore, we have to look for the reason why the threshold is as low as it is. It is the hypothesis that everyone is brought up to keep the rules that I shall call into question. I do not for a moment deny the importance of some of the factors I have mentioned. What I question is whether they operate uniformly on a homogeneously brought-up population.

The personal approach has received treatment recently from Talcott Parsons, and in what immediately follows I shall draw upon his work because I think it puts ideas with which we are fairly familiar in a new and interesting way. I shall then turn to the contribution to the subject made by R. K. Merton.

Let us consider the position of the child born into a given society. He is dependent principally on his mother, but societies differ in the degree of dependency. In some, like our own, he is dependent on a very restricted circle; in societies in which there are extended families, or elaborate kinship affiliations, he may have alternative comforters to whom he may go when in trouble. I believe that the terms in which the social rules are phrased may be connected with this. With us there is a special kind of internalization of values, together with an emphasis on obeying your conscience whatever other people say; when you have a group to please, it may be that emphasis is laid rather on getting group approval. A good deal of research needs to be done on this, but there seems to be evidence that societies differ in the way they convey the rules to succeeding generations.

However that may be, the child, as I have already said, is confronted with some version of the social rules mediated by the particular adults and coevals with whom he comes in contact. Broadly speaking, if he finds keeping the rules rewarding, he will keep them; if he finds his expectations dashed, then he will be placed in a conflict situation. This is one of the sources of deviance. Some writers think it the only source, but I shall suggest another.

Now, deviance is any departure from the acceptable range of conduct allotted to any position. It may take three forms: what the society calls illness, what the society calls delinquency, and what we may call "rebellion." Here we come up against a difficulty of classification. What a society calls "ill" at one time may be regarded as "delinquent" at another. What one society calls "ill," another may regard as worthy of high honour. Again, what some members of a society call delinquent and not ill, others may call "ill." And the rebel may not be considered a criminal in one society; in another he will. Nevertheless the distinctions, on the superficial level, are fairly clear. Roughly they are: those who would be classed as "ill" are those whose conduct does not correspond with some vague standard of rational expectation: those who are frightened without a reasonable cause, those who are unreasonably obsessed, the unduly elated, the unduly depressed, those whose suspiciousness passes ill-defined bounds, those who believe themselves to be the Pope, when everyone else thinks they are someone less exalted. We are prepared to think of motiveless crimes as coming into this category. The delinquents are those who have broken the law, with the exception of an admitted lunatic fringe.

The rebel is one who seeks to change society altogether. Whereas the criminal bases his conduct on *justifications* which we do not accept, the rebel bases his on *principles* which we do accept. The rebel claims that he is out for a better world, for a better society, for fairness to the oppressed, against selfishness, self-seeking, and greed— and are these values not values which we have all accepted? There is, as Parsons puts it, a bridge between the rebel and the society against which he rebels; there is no bridge between society and the criminal. So much for the superficial classification. The theoretical psychologist, however, confuses us. He wants to say that the same kind of conflict is responsible for delinquency as is responsible for what we regard as illness, and that the same compulsions are responsible for the rebel. I think there is much in this, but that it is by no means the whole story.

Talcott Parsons takes this line, and in doing so makes some valuable observations. To begin with, he distinguishes between disappointment with persons and disappointment with rules, between a sense of insecurity and a sense of inadequacy. Thus the child may look upon persons as his enemies, or on rule-keeping as a mug's game. He will cease to " care what they think " because caring has been unrewarding. However, in any case, he has learnt to regard conformity as a way to get rewards, even if it is by no means a sure way, and conforming has become part of himself—one of his acquired needs. On the other hand he is alienated. Thus there is a conflict between his need to conform and his alienative tendencies. This, says Parsons, leads to compulsive conduct. Either he will conform compulsorily for fear his alienative tendencies should get the upper hand, or he will behave with compulsive alienation as a reaction against his need to conform. He becomes aggressive, but compulsorily so; he is " agin the law," but compulsorily so; he is evasive of responsibility, but compulsorily so; he may be, if conformity is upper-most, conforming, but compulsorily so, thereby paving the way for deviance in those over whom he has control.

Now, why one man in his predicament should find his personal solution in illness, and another in delinquency, and a third in compulsive aggressive rebellion is not known. In the first case we may say that he turns his aggression inwards, in the second case he turns it out-wards, in the third case he cashes in on socially accepted grounds of resentment. Whether some constitutional peculiarity determines his choice—though, of course, he does not consciously choose—or whether the nature of his disillusionment is responsible, or whether the alternatives open to him are decisive, or whether (as is more likely) all three play their part, we do not at present know. Suffice it to say, at this juncture, that some become ill, some delinquent, and some rebels.

Now, Parsons' analysis fits in with a good deal of accepted opinion about mental illness; but what we want to know is what social factors predispose those subjected to them to choose one syndrome rather than another. Karen Horney has, indeed, in her *Neurosis of our Time* [1] given us some clues as to what features of our society are responsible for mental abnormality of some kind or another; but even in our own complex society one would suppose that people belonging to one section of it would be more prone to one form than people of another. The only research findings, so far as I am aware, concern the liability of officers in the army to suffer from obsessions while the rank and file suffered from hysteria when they were subjected to the strain of warfare. With this I must leave abnormality on one side.

So far as delinquency is concerned the case-history

[1] Kegan Paul, 1937.

studies with which we are familiar bring out the presence of underlying aggressive tendencies, and in many cases an element of compulsion (I think, for example, of the interpretations of Dr Stott).[1] Parsons makes the further point that the conformity element may find expression in delinquent gangs. These provide the best of both worlds—alienation and conformity—but are likely to be unstable because " not trusting " may be part of the de-linquent orientation.

In so far as this type of analysis, with its emphasis on conformity, applies to deviant movements which aim at changing the society, we might expect a kind of com-pulsive embittered aggression, while the element of conformity might perhaps be satisfied by an excessive pedantry with regard to the doctrine, making for in-group solidarity.

Now, this kind of personal approach is of value. It seeks to interpret deviance in the main by looking for the sources of tension and type of reaction in each deviant. It is readily admitted that the strains will vary from one social pattern to another, but it is not concerned, except indirectly, with the general features of societies which are likely to lead to deviance. Furthermore, I feel it lays too much stress on what might be called the pathological aspect of the individual deviant.

A welcome correction of the over-pathological approach is to be found in a recent publication: *Psychia-tric Aspects of Juvenile Delinquency* [2] by Dr L. Bovet. He observes that " of the 7,000 juveniles appearing before the Chicago juvenile courts, 705, or only 10%, were referred to psychiatric examination. Similarly in Lau-sanne, where there is a close collaboration between the juvenile courts and child psychiatrists, the average proportion of cases referred for medical and psychological

[1] *Delinquency and Human Nature* (Carnegie Trust, Dunfermline, 1950).
[2] World Health Organization, Geneva, 1951.

examination for the years 1947–1949 was 12% "
(p. 18). Now, of course, as Dr Bovet himself says, such
figures depend on the psychological sophistication of the
magistrates. There may certainly be more cases that
ought to have been referred. " Nevertheless," he says,
" a comparison between the total number of juvenile
delinquents and the number who show marked signs of
psychiatric or any other illness, seems to prove that the
majority of juveniles appearing for whatever reason before the juvenile courts or their equivalents, are medically
normal." He refers to the rise in the number of delinquents in recent years, and says that it is difficult to believe
that all of them were suffering from psychological disorders.
" A more plausible theory," he says, " is that this sudden
and temporary increase in juvenile delinquency is due to
external circumstances which affect the personality as an
accident might, rather than deeply, like an illness." It
is, indeed, the threshold story which he himself has introduced a few pages before that from which I have quoted.

More helpful is the approach of R. K. Merton in his
article on " Social Structure and Anomie." His view is
relatively simple. " It is my central hypothesis," he
says, " that aberrant behaviour may be regarded sociologically as a symptom of dissociation between culturally
prescribed aspirations and socially structured avenues for
realizing these aspirations." [1] Every society holds out
things worth striving for; it may be wealth, honour,
social service, or prowess as a warrior. Furthermore,
there are accepted methods of getting these ends. This,
however, works only if the people in whom these aspirations are engendered can realize them by the allowed
channels. Individual disappointments may occur, of
course, but that need not lead to any general debase-
ment of standards. Furthermore, there may be differential aspirations from one section of the society to

---

[1] *Social Theory and Social Structure*, p. 128.

another. Some may be led to aspire to wealth, others to honour, others to performing their duty in a more modest sphere. Provided there is general agreement on the different values which different groups aim at, and provided everyone in each group can satisfy his aspirations legitimately, then the rules which each group has to obey may be internalized in some way or other by its members, and collective pressure from the group itself and from society in general, in the form of expression of approval and disapproval, may preserve the pattern. The ideal type in each case is one who never dreams of aspirations other than those which he can, in fact, realize. With regard to other goals he may say: " Such are not for the likes of us."

Now, supposing there is a gap between aspiration and what is in fact attainable by legitimate means. Merton takes the case of America. There everyone aspires to wealth, and everyone is told that if he has the ability he can achieve what is held up as the thing most worth striving for. Indeed, he is made to feel guilty if he does not achieve it. And yet, in point of fact, except in very rare instances, achievement is impossible. There are forces at work which positively prevent his aspirations from being realized. Here, surely, we have what may fairly be called a contradiction between what people are told they can get, what they are encouraged to aim at, and what, in fact, is possible. This, says Merton, is a breeding ground of deviance. His analysis of the form it will take is not unlike that of Parsons, and I am not concerned with it. What seems to me important is to recognize that it affects whole sections of the community and not merely individual members of it. Leaving aside the political movements which aim at resolving the contradiction by changing the society, let us consider the field of delinquency. Those who cannot reach the goal by legitimate means will no longer take the rules seriously.

They may not question their legitimacy, but they will cease to have them so built into their system that they never think of infringing them. Nor will they pass them on to their children with the emphasis required for their incorporation.

The result will be a kind of doubling of standards. There will be the official standards and the standards of the sub-group to which you belong. Of course some sub-groups will have standards identical with the official ones, namely sub-groups whose aspirations can, on the whole, barring individual cases of ill luck, be realized by following prescribed lines. With the others, the official rules will remain, as it were, external to them. It may be, like the white-collar criminals described by E. H. Sutherland, that a sub-group emerges whose *de facto* agreed standards permit, and indeed almost require, their members to break the law. Business life for them is likened to a voyage in a sailing-ship; the technique is to sail as near the wind as you can. You do not deliberately break the rules for the fun of it, but if you do and get away with it—you're smart. On the other hand in the world from which most captured delinquents come, the law represents a hazard. Keeping the law is not a matter of right and wrong, though of course there are plenty of matters of right and wrong in such circles, but rather a matter of estimating risks. When my working-class friends talk about their plans, if it is a matter of breaking the law the question always is: "Is it worth it?" A young man came to see me the other day and told me that he had just got a job as driver of a coal lorry. He had replaced another man who had been caught delivering at his own house some of the coal that he should have delivered to his customers. My friend went on to say that the manager who set him on said to him, "Now don't you be a bloody fool; it's not worth risking the sack just for a couple of bob; if it were a hundred pounds, then I'd do it myself, but for a miserable couple of bob—NO." Of course pride is often taken in keeping the law: how often have I heard about the temptation to open the gas meter with a hairpin. " Quite easy," they say, " but I didn't. It wasn't worth the risk." The Governor of a Borstal once told me that all his boys thought of themselves as being " unlucky."

Now, in such a group the delinquent who takes the risk and gets " copped " is not necessarily actuated by complex compulsions. He may be, but I think myself that this quasi-pathological explanation is somewhat exaggerated. It is quite on the cards that none of the fashionable " causes " of crime is operative—broken homes, lack of love, and so forth. He may merely take risks which everyone else would if they were equally daring, or if they were equally silly. It is not so much that he deviates from his group, as that his group deviates from the official standards. And, note, it is not poverty as such that is the key, but rather that his aspirations, which are in accord with the official standards held up before him, cannot be satisfied in officially recognized ways. I would once more say that I am not suggesting that the section of society of which I am speaking have no standards at all. Of course they have. It is not at all surprising to me to hear that investigators have found that habitual criminals are scornful of accepting public assistance. In speaking of them as deviants from the official norm, I am not accusing them of mass criminality. I am not interested in those few who are, as they say, brought up to a life of crime. What I am saying is that with respect to making money, to getting hold of material goods, they tend to have a different attitude—if you like, a more practical one—than is the case with people whose *incorporated* standards are the same as the legal ones. Such people would, as we say, " not think " of doing this or that. The people of whom I am speaking think of it and, more often than not, reject it, because it is too risky. I should also add that I have exaggerated the picture. I have contrasted those who regard the law merely as an external barrier with those who have completely incorporated its rules. In fact, of course, the whole thing is more complicated. There are degrees of incorporation and there is selection in all groups of what precisely is incorporated and what is not. After all, many people who would not dream of infringing the law in any other way, may not have incorporated the rules about income tax.

Now, if this analysis is correct, and a good deal of research is needed into the standards of conduct of different groups, it means that delinquency will not be reduced by individual treatment, a matter to which I refer later; it will be reduced only if society is so transformed that what is held up as worth living for can be achieved by the majority of the population.

Another point also may be made. If this analysis is on the right lines, then it does not so much matter how complicated a social pattern may be, how detailed the regulations or role-playing, or—within limits—how much deprivation there is, that is to say, how much people have to forgo, provided the aspirations aroused are such as can be satisfied by legitimate conduct. The simpler peoples sometimes live a complex ritual life, like the Balinese mentioned before and the Zuni as described by Ruth Benedict. We may wonder how they stand for it. But if performing the ritual accurately is a socially recognized thing worth striving for, and if all who have that goal held up to them have their chance, then what we might think of as irksome need not be irksome at all. Social service might conceivably be a goal, a thing worth striving for, and material goods not of importance ; again, what we should regard as the self-sacrifice would not necessarily be frustrating provided one's aspirations could be satisfied; provided, that is to say, that one felt that what one was doing was in fact worth while. Now, as I have said, this hypothesis needs testing. We need a comparative study of societies with and without a high criminal rate to see whether this phenomenon of what Merton calls " anomie " can be detected elsewhere, and whether it is associated with the gap between aspiration and realization.

I am not denying the importance of case-history studies, or of the comparison between delinquent and non-delinquent groups. Nor do I deny that temperamental peculiarities may make life difficult when a given person's extract from the " arc of human potentialities " (as Ruth Benedict calls it) does not contain the potentialities favoured by the society into which he is initiated. Nor, again, do I deny the significance of traumatic incidents. All I am saying is that the more general social factors ought to be considered.

I am persuaded that the matter is of importance by reading the *Report of the Prison Commissioners for the Year 1951* (Cmd. 8692). At Stafford, a Young Prisoner Centre, the Governor reports a " surprising state of mind—numbers of lads to whom I have spoken about their future have said 'I hope I don't come back' almost as if they had no power of decision as to whether they would or not. . . . I very rarely hear what I used to hear in nearly every case when speculating about the future: ' No fear, I'm not coming back.' . . . Is it that the spirit of endeavour, self-respect and self-discipline have gone out of the lads, or are we simply getting the boys who are too weak to face up to things ? " Now I don't find this " state of mind " surprising in the least, and I venture to wonder whether the lads who made the approved reply were not merely more sensitive to the right kind of thing one ought to say to the Governor of a prison when taking one's leave.

Again, at the Allocation Centre at Wandsworth there was an elderly prisoner employed in the Officers' Mess. "He approached the Governor one day in great agitation. ' Sir, you will have to do something about Minnie (the mess cat)—she is a persistent thief ! ' He then launched into the details of the cat's thieving proclivities. It apparently had not occurred to him to do anything about the matter himself, any more than it had been borne in upon him to do anything about his own persistent thieving." Of course it hadn't. The case is admittedly paradoxical, but I should have been extremely surprised if he had taken his own thieving, in which he had been unlucky, as being on a par with that of the cat, which was personally exasperating.

Finally we have the evidence of a chaplain from a prison unknown. " I regret," he says, " that one can discern little signs of penitence among so many of the prisoners. It is very seldom indeed that a prisoner will say: ' I am going to give up crime because it is wrong and evil and a sin.' They will say that they are going to give it up, e.g. because the next time it will mean a long sentence of Preventive Detention etc " (p. 115).

I may, of course, be wrong, but I seem to detect a certain set of middle-class assumptions in these quotations, and a failure to recognize what life is like among other sections of the community—what sort of things are said, what standards are assumed. I would not dream of setting myself up as having more experience of delinquency than a prison Governor. My own experience has been gained through friendships with people who have regarded me as rather dull and backward, because of the naïve assumptions I make. I remember once going with one of my friends into a post office where I was given too much change. I handed back the difference, and when we came out my friend said: " Oh, Jack, where's your education ? " From such a small number it is, of course, impossible to generalize, but I am convinced that a study of deviant moral climates will prove at least as instructive as the study of individual deviants. We are, indeed, attempting something of the sort in a small town near Nottingham at the moment.

Of course, as I have said before, the whole question of the attitude of deviants towards their crimes raises the problem of treatment. Here I find myself in the difficulty in which I suppose we all are. If the deviant needs love, then love he must have, though I am well aware of the predicament of those who have withdrawn into hostility so far that they cannot be recalled. If, on the other hand, a great many potential deviants are simply deterred by the risk, then we ought to make the risk greater. Our penal institutions ought to be made less rather than more attractive, and that outrages our very reputable sense of decency. Of course a prison sentence as such is still, in many quarters, regarded as a social disgrace, but once the step has been taken, it is more like going into retreat—the brother of a friend of mine used to refer to the absences of my friend as " going on his holidays." Another man, who was in gaol for not paying a fine, came to see me after I had bought him out, and said: " I was just finishing a smashing book, when the Governor sent for me . . ." I felt I had timed it wrongly !

The alternative to making prison life less eligible is, presumably, to make life outside definitely more worth while. It is not easy to see how this is to be done, if the basic cause of the situation is as I have suggested— " anomie "—save by some change in the whole system whereby aspiration and possible achievement coincide. It may be that we must put up with our present delinquency rate as the rate appropriate to our civilization.

However that may be, let me return once more to the need for research. I have mentioned the need for

research into the thesis I have been elaborating. I should
like to add the need for research—this time personal research—into the effects of our present prison treatment
in all its various forms.   How many " normal " criminals
—if it is agreed that there are any—are changed charac-
ters after they have been through the treatment, so that,
whereas before they went in they contemplated crime as a
possible course of action, now they would not dream of
doing such a thing ?   How many of those who refrain
from criminal action after a spell " inside," do so because
they are deterred by the fear of a longer sentence ?   I
would not mind betting that the latter far exceed the
former.

Another topic of research is concerned with what I
believe to be uncharted regions. Granted that some
people are, as it were, driven to delinquency, as Dr
Stott will tell us, while others, as I suggest, regard the
law as something to be circumvented if you can, we may
ask whether the breaking of the law is random—determined merely by the circumstances in which the delinquent happens to find himself, or whether there are
what one might almost call institutionalized delinquent
patterns. Obviously technological development is important—the tommy-gun replaces the tent nail of Jael,
the wife of Heber the Kenite. This, however, is not
quite what I have in mind. What I have in mind is
this : If you are going to be a wide guy and take the risks
the mugs dare not take, what are you going to do ?
A very superficial survey of the scene would seem to
indicate that, besides taking every opportunity that may
offer—playing, one might say, on the nearest fiddle to
hand—delinquent conduct, like other conduct, tends to
be orchestrated. The *modus operandi*, as the police
records call it, is not merely a matter of personal whim,
it is a sub-socially accepted role, with or without sub-
cultural prestige. The cosh-boy, the gangster, the

" snow-drop " who pinches the laundry, the " tiger " who pinches doormats, occupy delinquent *positions* in society—and there are many others. Kleinburg points out that immigrant delinquents tend to take over the delinquent pattern characteristics of the American way of life.

What I am suggesting is that in some sense, a social system not only precipitates its own delinquency rate, but that it also standardizes to a certain extent the forms which delinquency will take.

CHAPTER VII

The Grand Manner

IN the third chapter I was mainly dealing with actual social research and its variety. I did, however, mention the general problem of social theory. I was concerned there with the problem of establishing what might be called the rules of integration. This is not the only form that large-scale social theorizing takes. One of the roots of sociology, to quote Professor Ginsberg, " is the philosophy of history, which in modern times has generally been an attempt in the grand manner to inter- pret the whole course of human history as part of a wider philosophical world view. From this sociology may be said to have arisen by way of reaction against sweeping generalization unsupported by detailed in- quiry." [1] The attempt to establish very general rules of historical development is what Professor T. H. Marshall calls " the way to the stars," [2] and he warns us against it, or at any rate those of us who do not carry the vast range of knowledge, which is required for such an enterprise, in our knapsacks. But the stars are always tempting, and I want to try to consider how near we can get to them.

This is a very large subject, and all I will do now is to put one or two points before you which seem to me to be important.

I am going to start at a very elementary level: the actual putting forward, receiving, accepting, or rejecting of what might be called sociologico-historical hypotheses.

[1] *Sociology* (Home Univ. Library, 1934), p. 25.
[2] *Sociology at the Crossroads* (LSE, 1947).

What happens is that an hypothesis is put forward and it is accepted or rejected according to agreed criteria of acceptability. These will vary from time to time according to the prevailing standards of what is deemed to be knowledge, and according to criteria that are deemed to be relevant to the kind of hypothesis under consideration. If two people differ about the criteria that are relevant, or about what other things they believe to be true, then further discussion becomes impossible. There is no " peep behind the scenes " to see which is right. There are standard ways of trying to convince by argument and evidence, but there is no direct look at something called " reality " which enables us to decide between one hypothesis and another. There are, to be sure, standard rules of falsification according to which if deductions from an hypothesis lead to expectations which are not realized, then the hypothesis as it stands is to be rejected by those who abide by such rules. There might, however, be cases where an hypothesis, which would be rejected under that set of rules, is nevertheless retained because those rules are not seriously applied.

Now, the application of sociological thought to historical development may take a variety of forms which, for the sake of convenience, I will call " the interpretation of historical events," the " attempt to establish general laws," and the " active interest in changing society." These are not mutually exclusive; the same person may be interested in all three, but I think it is important to notice that the different emphases are connected with different criteria of validity. I propose to consider them in turn.

We all live in a world with a past. We have, as it were, a picture of ourselves and the events happening about us as being at the end of a long series of happenings recorded for us by historians. We want to know why these events took place as they did. We may look for a universal pattern into which everything can be fitted—

that is my second approach. We may, on the other hand, take sets of events, chunks of recorded history, and seek to understand or interpret them. Hypotheses are put forward, in the first place, about what actually happened, and criteria are brought to bear on the actual value of the evidence itself. The standard criteria will vary from age to age. At one time reports coming down to us from the past will be taken at their face value, at another they will be scrutinized for political bias. The dating of documents may be influenced by changing opinion about language and style. And so on. But supposing the account of the facts is acceptable, then we ask *why* they happened like that. More hypotheses are put forward. They may be hypotheses about the decision-making of men in strategically important positions. We accept or reject them according to our general ideas about what people are like. Such ideas, again, vary from age to age. What would be called " far-fetched " in one age is taken for granted in another. Unconscious motivation is now a commonplace. With such psychological explanation we may be contented. It depends on (1) the question asked, and (2) the sort of thing we believe to be important.

If we think, as nowadays we do, because our attention has been drawn to them, that what we vaguely call " social factors " are important, then we shall not be satisfied with psychological answers about individuals, and also we shall be interested in different questions. We shall ask what the political and economic situations were in which decisions were made, or we shall demand that history be written in terms of the political and/or economic predicaments of groups. The history of Athens now becomes intelligible, not in terms of the personal characteristics of Solon, Pisistratus, or Clisthenes, but in terms of the economic developments and consequent political alignments of which they were the representative figures.[1] We are now interested in such things as the fate of the middle classes in Germany as compared with the fate of the *bourgeoisie* in France. We learn from Dr Elias [2] that in Germany they were kept out of political affairs and therefore took to romanticism and *innigkeit* as a reaction against the sophisticated courts; while in France they were brought into the world of affairs and took, instead, to enlightenment. And what convinces us ? What makes the interpretation ring true or false ? Is it not, *au fond*, again a matter of our estimate of human nature ? We now believe that individual men are conditioned by their social environment; we further believe that economic factors are the most significant features of that environment. What Popper calls our " horizons of expectation " are enlarged so as to include such matters, and we accept interpretations which fit them, and reject those that do not. We are sophisticated enough to know that people are not always aware of their own motivations, and that they think they are acting for the good of their country while really, in some sense of " really," they are furthering the interests of their class. But I think the ultimate justification for historical interpretation is an appeal to some consensus of opinion about human nature. Of course there are other considerations as well: there are the environmental facts, the numerical estimation of the population, their skills, and the material resources at their disposal. But when we say we *understand* what happened, it seems to me that what we are saying is that the explanation offered tallies with what is at any time the common sense. We are not dealing with the establishment of laws, but with the application of such very general laws about human nature as we believe to have been established. However, I think this is often what is meant when it is

[1] cf. G. Thomson, *Æschylus and Athens* (Lawrence and Wishart, 1941).
[2] *Uber Den Prozess der Zivilisation*, Falken (Basel, 1939).

said that in order to understand any social state of affairs one must consider the historical events that led up to it.

Now the second type of task people have set themselves is the establishment of laws of historical development, or at any rate the establishment of laws of human interaction which apply not to the small-scale problems I have discussed in previous chapters but rather to social events in a wider sense. Can one, it is asked, by inspecting the course of history, detect the operation of laws ? One school of thought, exemplified by Troeltsch, seems to deny such a possibility on principle. For him we have to make an intuitive grasp of individuals, societies, or groups as unique and unrepeatable wholes, and this bars the application to them of the analysis and comparisons which scientific treatment involves. I see no grounds for accepting such a theory. I should have thought that it would in fact render communication about societies impossible, and I do not think this is the case. Furthermore, when Troeltsch himself writes about religion and other social phenomena, he does seem to me to use the same kinds of criteria of validity that are commonly accepted.

Granted, then, that there is no bar to scientific treatment in the nature of our knowing about history, what kinds of rules can we hope to discover ? One form which the most grandiose scheme takes is the attempt to detect a pattern of historical change into which the whole history of mankind, or very large pieces of it, can be fitted. We have, for instance, cyclical theories like that of Spengler, with his eight high cultures, each with its own prime symbol, and each passing through the same phases ending in civilization and collapse; or that of Toynbee, with his challenge and the response of the creative minority, their loss of creativity, followed by the world State with its internal and external proletariat who overthrow it. We also have more general unilinear patterns like those of Comte and Spencer. Each author, with the great rolls of history before him, so far as he knows it, has noted certain similarities looming through the mass of differences as he casts his eye from age to age or from one area of the globe to another. Or else, perhaps, he has seen features which have struck him in the study of one section of the rolls—say the history of the Roman Empire—and he has looked for similar features elsewhere.

Moreover, it must be admitted that there is a certain amount of agreement among theorists of this kind. Sorokin has recently made a comparative study of seven writers who have attempted to detect large-scale patterns in history. Danilevsky, Spengler, and Toynbee think in terms of the life-cycles of civilizations; Schubart, Berdyaev, Northrop, and Sorokin himself think rather in terms of what Sorokin calls " cultural super-systems," which succeed one another. There are, however, curious parallels between the phases distinguished by the first group and the super-systems noted by the second. Thus, the characteristics of the early phase of a civilization—its childhood or its creative period—resemble those characteristics which distinguish Sorokin's " ideational " type, Schubart's " ascetic-messianic " type, Berdyaev's " barbaric-religious " type, and Northrop's " dominantly æsthetic " type. The characteristics of maturity are similar to the type of culture which Sorokin calls " idealistic," Schubart " harmonious," and Berdyaev " medieval-renaissance." Finally, the period of decline, in which they all agree that we are now living, is an age which Sorokin calls " sensate " culture, Schubart " heroic or Promethean," Berdyaev " humanistic-secular," and Northrop " predominantly theoretic." Furthermore, according to Spengler, the decline of a culture is marked by the emergence of what he calls the " second religiosity," which corresponds to Toynbee's " new universal church

and religion " ; while Sorokin looks for a return of " idea-
tion " to replace the existing " sensate " culture.   As to
where the new civilization is to emerge, there is some
difference of opinion.   Danilevsky, Spengler, and Schubart look for it in Eurasia and Russia, while Sorokin
considers " the vast region of the Pacific as the territorial
centre and the Americas, India, China, Japan and Russia
as the leading players in the coming drama of the emerging
integral or ideational culture." [1]   The one thing that is
perhaps of interest to the sociologist is, I think, that
writers approaching history from many different points
of view, seem to agree about the cultural differences
which distinguish one age from another.   This seems to
me to point to a certain coherence of cultural products at
any given time—a point to which I shall refer later.   The
type of explanation they give raises the issue of the type
of explanation which satisfies scientific criteria.

It is important to recognize that these writers are
making historical statements.   They are saying: these
recurrences or this sequence did take place.   They are
not providing us with any laws.   They may give the
impression of doing so because we have a tendency, when
a cyclical pattern or a directional series is put before us,
to suppose that there is something which makes the one
go round, as it were, and the other go forward.   It looks
somehow as though there were some inner force pro-
pelling it.   Now, a law is of the form of a universal
proposition: whenever you have x you have y.   It may
be deduced from a body of theory or it may be an empirical generalization; and in order to test it you must
be able to detect cases of x and cases of y.   *A trend is
not a law.*[2]   The decline of the birthrate is not a law and
we can only decide whether the trend will continue in

---

[1] *Social Philosophies of an Age of Crisis* (A. & C. Black, 1952), p. 298.
[2] Cf. " The Poverty of Historicism," by K. Popper, *Economica*, Vol.
XII, 1945, p. 72.

the same direction if we know the laws which are responsible for each item of the series being what it was. We cannot extrapolate unless we are entitled to assume that the same conditions operate now as operated in the past. Similarly with all patterns of development; if they are to be more than entertaining ways of organizing human history they must be analysed into the laws which operated at every stage. We must know, for instance, what characterizes, say, a challenge, what characterizes a response, and what characterizes a creative minority. Then we can proceed to look for all cases which satisfy the conditions of " challenge," and all cases in which we have such conditions, combined with the presence of people who fit the criteria for " creative minority," and then see whether the reaction was characterized by the hall-marks of " response," whatever these may be. We might then consider whether the " response " state of affairs ever occurred in the absence of the conditions which define " challenge " or those which define the " creative minority " or both. If challenge, creative minority, and response were always found together, and if the response never occurred in the absence of the other two, then, at any rate, the rule would not so far be falsified.

So far as I know, this careful formulation and testing has not occupied the minds of those who have attempted to portray the forces responsible for human history, with the possible exception of Sorokin. He did at least attempt to establish what he calls the " logico-meaningful " integration of his three types of human cultures: the " ideational," the " idealistic," and the " sensate," by a tremendously laborious collection of specimens of art, literature, philosophies, political doctrines, and economic attitudes, which he thought characteristic of each type, and which flourished more or less together when that type was ascendant.

Such detailed procedure is, however, rare. This complaint has recently been voiced by L. F. Richardson.[1] In Toynbee's *Study of History* he says, "Events are described but seldom counted, nor does the chi-squared test appear." Richardson, himself, has collected details of all the wars that broke out between 1820 and 1929, and arranged them in order of deadliness by calculating how many people were killed in them. He has arranged them in order of magnitude, defining " magnitude " as " the logarith to the base ten of the number of persons who died because of that quarrel." He then worked out the frequency of such quarrels of different magnitudes during the period. The result: " the larger the fewer " is not surprising, but at any rate it is reached by careful counting. More interesting are his calculations concerning the number of outbreaks of war in any year between 1820 and 1929, a calculation, also applied to the material collected by Wright in his " Study of War," which covers the period 1500–1931. In both cases the series of numbers obtained by taking the number of years in these periods in which no wars broke out, one war, two wars, three wars, four wars, corresponds closely to what would be the case if wars broke out in accordance with a " Poisson distribution " based on the assumption that the probability that some war would break out on a day is very small and is the same for each day. It is not easy to see what the implication of all this is. Richardson suggests that " the Poisson distribution draws attention to a persistent probability of change from peace to war or from war to peace, perhaps due to the fact that discontent with present conditions underlies even the high purposes of peace and war." [2]

[1] *Brit. J. of Sociol.*, Vol. III, 1952, p. 77.
[2] " Statistics of Deadly Quarrels," from *Psychological Factors of Peace and War*. Ed. Pear (Hutchinson, 1950).

From the instances I gave above of the kind of procedure which is necessary if any social laws are going to be established, you will see that it is a formidable business. I am not saying that the task is impossible, I am merely saying that the knowledge and research required are enormous. Let me take an example. Here is an hypothesis from an interesting piece of historical research into the relation between military organization and social structure carried out by a young Pole called Andrzeejwski. "The predominance of attack over defence tends to diminish the number of independent governments within a given area and to widen the areas under their control and/or facilitates the tightening of control over the areas already under their domination; while the superiority of defence tends to produce opposite results." [1] Such an hypothesis is in principle verifiable or falsifiable, but the amount of research would be very great. Similarly with rules relating matrilinearity to patrilinearity, economic structure to belief, methods of production to relations of production, and so on. The trouble with such generalizations as are put forward is, I think, that their authors rest their case upon a few favourable instances, and do not set out to see whether there are any negative ones.

The instances I have mentioned so far have been cases in which the attempt is made or might be made to establish empirical uniformities. In the case, however, of dialectical and historical materialism the position, if I understand it rightly, is different. Here we have a theory from which uniformities could in principle be deduced. The phenomena of Nature, which includes societies, are apprehended " as being in constant movement and undergoing constant change, and the development of Nature as the result of the development of the contradictions in Nature are the result of the interaction of opposed forces

[1] *Military Organization and Society*, Kegan Paul (1954).

in Nature." [1]   The process of development passes from
insignificant quantitative changes to open, fundamental
changes, to qualitative changes; it is a development in
which the qualitative changes occur not gradually, but
rapidly and abruptly, taking the form of a leap from one
state to another.   In society the determining force is the
method of procuring the means of life together with
men's relations of production—co-operation, domination,
and subordination and the like.   Methods of production
must form a serial order because later methods imply the
existence of former ones.   These productive methods
have appropriate relations of production attached to
them, but there is often a lag in changes of the latter to
correspond with changes in the former.   Such a state
of affairs is an instance of contradiction.   However, it is
also the case that: " No social order ever perishes before
all the productive forces for which there is room in it
have developed." [2]   During this period, presumably as
the quantitative changes are mounting up, new social
ideas and theories develop, " force their way through,
become the possession of the masses, mobilize and
organize them against the moribund forces of society,
and then facilitate the overthrow of these forces, which
hamper the development of the material life of the
society."   Social change throws its shadow beforehand,
and therefore " we must not base our orientation on the
strata of society which are no longer developing but on
strata which are developing and have a future before
them, even though they at present do not constitute the
predominant force." [3]   Armed with this theoretical
structure, the science of the history of society " can
become as precise a science as, let us say, biology." [4]

With one fundamental reservation I see no objection,

[1] *Dialectical and Historical Materialism*, by J. Stalin (Moscow, 1950), p. 7.
[2] *Critique of Political Economy*, by Marx.   Quoted Stalin, op. cit. p. 56.
[3] Stalin, op. cit. p. 15.   [4] ibid., p. 23.

provided the theory satisfies obvious scientific criteria; I think, however, there are difficulties which the theory will have to overcome. For example: " All Nature is a process of change, and," says Lenin, " dialectics is the study of the contradiction within the very essence of things." For the theory to be scientifically established it is clear that we must know how to recognize a contradiction. We are told that the lag between modes of production and relations of production is an instance, but that does not carry us very far. What, for example, was the contradiction in what is described as primitive communism ? What is the (or are the) contradiction which is within the very essence of the USSR today, and what will it be when communism is established ? Again, all change involves the rhythm of quantitative change, a leap, and qualitative change. The leap, one gathers, in society, is of the order of a revolution. It follows that we must be able to detect the sudden leaps from primitive communism to a slave society, and from a slave society to feudalism, which seem to occur when new methods of production are invented. I have no doubt that it can be established, but so far I must confess I have not come across the evidence. Clearly *all* cases must be considered. It is no use taking a few favourable instances. As I understand it the qualitative change must always be sudden. Has it always been sudden ? And what is the criteria of " sudden " ? We are warned by Mao Tse-Tung, in his pamphlet *On Contradiction*, that contradiction does not imply antagonism, and he quotes Lenin to that effect: " Antagonism and contradiction," says Lenin, " are utterly different. Under Socialism, antagonism disappears, but contradiction exists." Thus Mao says : " Economically, in capitalistic society (where the town under *bourgeoisie* rule ruthlessly exploits the countryside) and in the Kuomintang-ruled areas in China (where the town under the rule of foreign imperialism and the native comprador, big *bourgeoisie* most savagely exploits the countryside) the contradiction between the town and the countryside is one of extreme antagonism. But in a Socialist country and in our revolutionary bases, such an antagonistic contradiction becomes a non-antagonistic contradiction; and it will disappear when a communist society is realized." [1]   This was written in 1937. What one wants to know is whether the law of sudden change holds for non-antagonistic-contradiction as it appears to do for antagonistic ones. Or is a policy of gradual winning over possible? Again, how does one judge whether the production forms in a society have developed to their full capacity? Change will not occur until this is the case. We cannot, clearly, be satisfied with a *post facto* assertion that a given social order must have reached its full capacity of production, otherwise it would not have perished. And, lastly, how can we detect the developing strata on which Stalin bade us base our orientation? Not after they have proved successful. To be of any value in prediction we must be able to detect them when they do not constitute the predominant force.

Such are the questions which I think would have to be answered if *Dialectical and Historical Materialism* is to meet the criteria of scientific validity. Some of them were answered in Stalin's last address on the economic situation in the USSR, but I do not think that all the difficulties I have mentioned are fully appreciated.

However, it might be objected that such a theory is not concerned with such rules of inference at all. In Stalin's *Dialectical and Historical Materialism* we note constant reference to practical activity. "In order not to err in policy," he says, "we must look forward, not backward." Since abrupt qualitative change is a law of development "one must be a revolutionary, not a reformist." Surely,

[1] *On Contradiction* (Foreign Language Press, Pekin, 1952), pp. 68–69.

it might be said, all this laborious formulation of hypotheses in a testable form, and then pursuing verification
throughout the whole range of history so that no negative instance, if any, could escape, surely that is the most
wearisome waste of time. This theoretical structure, it
might be said, is the product of those very new social
forces of which it speaks, propounded by those who had a
clearer view of their destiny. It is not a set of reflections
about the process of change; it is an instrument of that
very process. The criteria to apply are the pragmatic
ones of acceptance and success. Such is the third type of
validity of which I spoke at the beginning of this chapter.
And one point of importance to sociologists is that many
prophecies or predictions are, as it were, self-realizing.
The very fact of their being uttered influences the events
about which they make utterance.

And now I want to come back to the reservation I
mentioned in connection with the possibilities of testing
the inferences to be drawn from *Dialectical and Historical
Materialism*. My reservation does not apply only to
these, it applies also to all attempts to establish social
laws on this large scale. It is, I think, fundamental. I
am prepared to agree that it might be possible to formulate
and test large-scale generalizations, provided one had the
requisite knowledge of history. They would be difficult
to verify in such a way as to give them a high probability
value, but let us not worry about that. What I do not
think you can hope to do is to provide rules about those
very agencies of change which we would like to be able
to predict: episodic inventions and decisions. Supposing you knew all the social rules which apply to, say,
a Bronze-Age culture, and supposing you knew the rules
that will come into force when iron is discovered, you
cannot know from the first when—or even *that*—the
second will come into operation. And this goes for
all inventions which are utilized in new methods of

production. You may be able to foresee what will happen *if* an invention is made, but your rules will not enable you to deduce *that* the invention will, in point of fact, be made at all. The same, I would say, is true about innovations in the moral and political world. I cannot see from what social rules the existence of Marx could have been predicted. If it is said that some spokesman of the new order would be bound to arise, I would ask whether it could be predicted that he would be a student of Hegel, and if not whether the theory propounded might have been different in material respects. I would say the same about decision-making. If we knew the social rules operating at the present time, I do not see how we could predict the decisions which will be made by Malenkov and Eisenhower during the next year. On these grounds, I think, the kind of predictions we are likely to be able to make are short-term ones, and ones of limited scope.

This does not mean that the application of theoretical analysis in the grand manner is useless. We may not be able to predict what is likely to happen, but we might be able to formulate certain limits to the variety which is possible.

In the first place there are what one might call " constitutive limits." In the field of demography, for example, we can set limits to the growth of population by calculating the number of female children who survive to child-bearing age, and by making alternative predictions on a variety of assumptions about the number of children they are likely to have. We can set limits to the number of people who can be provided with a standard number of calories under existing and, on the basis of our present knowledge, more possible methods of agricultural production. We can set limits to industrial production on the basis of our knowledge of the availability of raw materials and sources of power. All this, however, as the last example reminds us, can be done only if we assume that no method of child production other than that known to us will be discovered, or that the scientists will not find out ways of feeding us quite different from those with which we are familiar.

Secondly, we might be able to work out certain formal incompatibilities in the field of role-values, in the way Talcott Parsons suggests. On his scheme the universalistic, specific, affectively neutral, achievement oriented roles are incompatible with a large-scale kinship structure. Again, a dominantly collectivity-oriented system is incompatible with a privately-oriented system, such as China.

Thirdly, there are what one might call " psychophysiological imperatives." Every social system must satisfy certain basic needs of its members. The trouble here is that beyond such obvious needs as the provision of sufficient nourishment we hardly know what these basic needs are. If, however, we could get some agreed criteria of what is pathological, we might be able to find out what pressures different role-systems bring to bear upon their actors, and what compensatory reliefs they are likely to seek. Parsons, for instance, suggests that the affective-neutrality and achievement pattern is incompatible with close ties of community solidarity, which are inevitably diffuse rather than specific. " Perhaps," says Parsons, " partly as a compensatory mechanism in this context, such societies tend to develop intense diffuse affective attitudes of solidarity with reference to the largest unit of community, namely the nation." Are we to suppose that the need to express affection is such that if the major roles in a society do not afford opportunity, then some way out will be found ?

Fourthly, there are structural imperatives. With the elaboration of the division of labour there is an inherent tendency to differentiate along two axes, both of which have inferiority–superiority implications. The first is the axis of competence, the second the axis of responsibility, where division of labour is so complicated that it demands organization. Obviously facilities will be differentially distributed. This means that there will be a stratification in terms of competence and responsibility. Now, is it true, as Parsons declares, that " it is literally impossible to have an instrumental system sanctioned by the valuation of achievement without the internal differentiation of the role and facility structure coming *also* to be a differentiation of rewards, an internal stratification " ? And if there is some kind of family life will it not be impossible for " the wives and children of those high and low in the occupational system to be equally treated, *regardless of their personal achievement* " ? If this is the case, " the combination of an occupationally differentiated industrial system and a significantly solidary kinship system *must* be a system of stratification in which the children of the more highly placed come to have differential advantages " (*Social System*, p. 161). Besides stratification, the study of the requirements of organization itself, the study of intercommunication, both vertical and horizontal, will enable us to set limits to possible variety. Again " no society can subsist unless there is a basis of ' counting on ' some control of the use of force," and the form this will take will partly be dependent on the technology of armaments.

Finally Parsons suggests that there must be some system of beliefs which will serve to explain the inevitable discrepancy between " institutionally legitimized expectations and the actual outcome of events " (p. 164). Such an explanation is not a mere scientific account, which may satisfy the curious, it is rather to serve as a consolation to the bewildered. Hitherto religion has been the opium; the interesting question is whether those for whom religious formulations no longer serve require something to take its place.

The precise form that social systems will take will obviously depend upon the detailed series of events of which they are the outcome at any given moment of history. The function of social theory in the field of historical change is not to prophesy the future, but rather to work out the limitations within which future developments are likely to occur.

Whether, in view of the formidable size of the task, social scientists ought to attempt it, is really a rather foolish question. The fact is that some of them undoubtedly will. What is important is that they should do it properly. The way to the stars is long, painful, and dreary. Let us not be deceived into thinking we are setting out in that direction, when we are really rocketing forth into the empty spaces of journalism.

CHAPTER VIII

The Sociology of Knowledge

THIS topic, the sociology of knowledge, is difficult to define with any precision. It is concerned with the way in which systems of thought, whether cognitive or evaluative or both, are conditioned by other social facts. It can be tackled in at least two ways. You can study actual systems of thought or evaluative attitudes in the population in which you live, in order to see whether they vary as you pass from one group to another, and how they can be changed. This is the American approach. The European approach is different. There the whole range of human thought as it has come down to us, together with the thoughts of preliterate peoples, is analysed, and characteristically different systems of ideas are related to their appropriate social structures, and to other systems of ideas with which they must cohere. This opens up a vast field for speculation, and it must be admitted that the bright ideas that are put before us are often not backed up by any further investigation which might produce evidence to support them or refute them. The American approach often seems somewhat trivial, the European approach all too conjectural. As Merton tartly remarks, the former march under a banner with the motto: " We don't know that what we say is particularly significant, but at least it is true "; the latter raise high the banner which reads: " We don't know that what we say is true, but it is at least significant." [1]

[1] *Social Theory and Social Structure*, p. 199.

I shall not be concerned with the American studies of opinion, attitude, and mass-communication, though I think their methods might be employed to study some of the theoretical problems which I shall raise. I propose rather to consider some of the European contributions in order to see how far they can be made the subject of social scientific research.

In a simple sense we can say that systems of cognitive belief and evaluation are socially conditioned because without social interaction there would be no such systems at all. Without language, systems of thought cannot exist, and without social interaction there is no language. Every human group, as I said in the first chapter, develops beliefs and values which are given communicable form in symbolic registration. These systems of beliefs and values are passed on from generation to generation, and develop a quasi-independence of their own, so that they confront the new-comer as something over against him, something which he must accept, a set of terms in which his own individual point of view must be expressed. Without such agreed terms, communication is impossible, and without communication, human social systems, as we know them, cannot persist. Furthermore, these systems cannot be derived from the intentions and motives of the particular person who operates them at any given time. A man may act in terms of an accepted set of values because he feels them to be right, or because he fears the consequences of infringing them, or because he seeks prestige by behaving in accordance with them.

Since interaction precipitates belief, systems, and normative principles, one would readily accept that different systems of interaction would precipitate different systems and principles. There must, however, be certain limits to the variety. A great deal of the content of cognitive systems is concerned with the manipulation of the environment, both physical and biological, including human. A considerable amount of lore must be accumulated which is common to all societies, and this will be registered in language which can be translated from one set of symbols to another. The social anthropologist can understand the Trobriand Islander when he describes the making of a canoe, the planting of his yams, and the method adopted in fishing because what one might call their immediate view of what Nature is like is the same as his. When it comes to values, one might expect, and, indeed, one finds, vast differences in content, from one social system to another, but here again one must not exaggerate. Evaluation itself is common to all social systems, and evaluative symbols are translatable even though the content valued will vary from one context to another. And, as has been pointed out by students of comparative ethics, certain moral approvals and disapprovals are prerequisites for the very persistence of interactive groups. There would seem to be a central core of regard for the interests of others, though who the others are will doubtless vary from one society to another. It is noteworthy that in our own day, when opinions and attitudes differ violently from one group to another, according, so it is alleged, to class interests, all groups justify their policies in terms of the same system of values. The point is that although there are considerable differences in cognitive systems and moral codes, the very fact that translation from one language to another is possible, and even the fact that some words are intelligible but not translatable, shows that the range of varieties is limited. Of course we may often be wrong in our translation, but if we can have any intercourse at all with people whose social structures differ so widely from our own, and if we can give a coherent, and partially verifiable, account of past ages from the documents and inscriptions they have left behind, our translations cannot be wholly false.

However, although there is basic agreement from one set of humans to another about how certain parts of Nature can be manipulated, there is considerable difference of view about what Nature is like, and about how investigations should proceed; and attempts have been made to relate these different views to other features of the societies in which they are held. Our own preoccupation with the social conditioning of ideas, for example, is—as Mannheim has pointed out—the resultant of the clash of opinions in a social context in which there is no universally accepted body of doctrines.

As to views that are held regarding the nature of the world about us, Durkheim held that the very categories of our thought are derived from social intercourse: " the category of class started by being indistinguishable from the idea of a human group; it is the rhythm of social life that lies at the basis of the category of time; it is the spatial arrangement of society which provides the category of space," [1] and in support of the last hypothesis he quotes the case of the Zuni, whose dwelling space is occupied by seven groups of clans, and who therefore divide space into seven regions. This again is supported by Granet, who tells us that the ancient Chinese did not believe in empty space and time, but rather in four differentiated regions, each with its colour, its season, and its virtues. This, he says, is a reflection from the feudal assembly, at which the vassals formed a square, each side with its appropriate colour, and each group standing on the side nearest to the direction from which it had come. Every four years the vassals came to the centre, and on the fifth year the chief visited the four regions at the appropriate season. [2] Kelsen in his *Society and Nature* [3] holds that " the fundamental principle which determines primitive man's behaviour towards

---

[1] *Formes Elementaires de La Vie Religieuse* (Paris, 1925), p. 628.
[2] *La Pensée Chinoise* (Paris, 1934), pp. 93–95.   [3] Kegan Paul, 1946, p. 49.

Nature is the same as that which decides his conduct towards the members of his own and other groups—the social principle of retribution."

Again, a Marxist writer, Maurice Cornforth, holds that " it was typical of the natural philosophy of the feudal period that everything in Nature was explained in terms of its proper place in the system of the universe," [1] while the *bourgeoisie* philosopher regarded Nature as a system of bodies in interaction, their atomic theories being, it would appear, a reflection of an individualistic economic régime.

And academician K. M. Bykov, addressing the Scientific Session on the Physiological Teachings of Pavlov, observed: " Like every other science, ' psychosomatic medicine ' is based upon a definite philosophical foundation, which is a reflection of definite social and class relations in society. And, depending upon this philosophical foundation, any given science develops either along the path of true science or along the path of pseudoscience. The aim of the latter in class society is to protect the interests of the doomed class to fulfil its social orders, and thereby ' fence itself off from the people.' Abroad, especially in America, where the expansionist tendencies of monopoly capitalism are manifested in their most brazen form, ' psychosomatic medicine ' is forced to arm itself with the most reactionary theories in order to defend the interests of the ruling classes. These theories are couched in terms of instincts of aggression, and, though notice is taken of the high incidence of psychosomatic complaints in the urban Negro population, no mention is made of the exploitation that is responsible for it. Instead of the American term ' psychosomatics ' which stresses the dualistic view, it would be more correct from the medical aspect to designate this field as corticovisceral pathology."

[1] *Dialectical Materialism* (Lawrence and Wishart, 1952), p. 38.

Such correspondence theories are, one would think, verifiable by an exhaustive investigation of social structure and the theories about Nature held within them. It would be an enormous enterprise, and would have to be preceded by an analysis into what formal features are to count as a basis of correspondence; but until it is carried out we are left with a few suggestive hints of little scientific value.

Another way in which cognitive systems are said to be conditioned is through the agency of some principle of compatibility between one set of ideas and another. Thus Dr Needham in his Hobhouse Memorial Lecture on " Human Law and the Laws of Nature in China," tells us that the idea of laws of Nature which can be discovered could not have developed in China. It derived in the West from a development of the idea of law in the judicial sense, and from the notion of God as a lawgiver, while in China there was no theological stage. Conduct and harmony were all important, and " the harmonious co-operation of all beings . . . arose from the fact that they were all parts in a hierarchy of wholes forming a cosmic pattern and what they obeyed were the internal dictates of their own natures." In such a climate science in the western sense could not be born. Similarly, Max Weber has tried to show that capitalism could not develop in China because of the entrenched traditionalism of the *élite*; nor in India because of an other-worldly outlook which questioned the very existence of the world of sense; nor among the Jews because of their pre-occupation with the Covenant. In Europe, on the other hand, the climate of opinion and the break from tradition were congenial to the development of capitalism and to the establishment of a scientific attitude, as Merton[1] has shown in his study of the influence of Puritanism on the rise of science.

[1] *Social Theory and Social Structure*, p. 329.

These compatibility theories make their initial appeal to inspection. Is this view compatible with that ? We, as thinking creatures, recognize compatibility when we see it. It is a matter of understanding, and differs from the last type of social conditioning. There is nothing inherently incompatible in a tribe which groups its huts in a circle, thinking of the universe as square. The theoretical problem is: to what extent is it possible for incompatible beliefs to be held in logic-tight compartments without causing intolerable strain ?

A third line of thought, rather overlapping with the last, relates scientific inquiry to the needs of the age. Scientific inquiry, as Dr Needham suggests, may be ruled out by an incompatible climate of opinion. It may be stifled, as Professor Farrington [1] tells us, when the creative artificers, from whose activities science springs, are replaced by slaves, whose work is held to be beneath notice by the slave-owning class. These then indulge in what is, by contrast, deemed to be pure thought. When, however, the *bourgeoisie* break the bonds of feudalism and question the dogmas of religion, when individual initiative is prized and individual freedom of thought is claimed, and when new opportunities of industry and commerce present themselves, then the institutionalization of science becomes possible. Now scientific inquiry can be discussed from two points of view: content and form. The former is simple enough. New developments in trade and industry and, we might add, war, set new problems for scientific investigation. Thus, a study of scientific thought in the seventeenth century shows the influence of practical problems of navigation on the actual topics investigated by the scientists of the day. The problems, for instance, of finding the longitude and determining the times of the tides occupied the minds of the early members of the Royal Society. It is obvious that

[1] *Greek Science* (Penguin).

economic and commercial problems are of outstanding importance in influencing what scientists will do their science about. However, a careful inquiry by Merton into the socio-economic influence on the selection of problems discussed by the members of the Royal Society in 1661–62 and 1686–87 shows that 58·7 per cent were related to socio-economic needs, and the remaining 41·3 per cent were not.[1] Scientists may derive from technicians, but the role of scientists in the *bourgeoisie* world is not the same as the role of technicians. The institutionalization of science, as we understand it, means the establishment of a code of standards. Freedom of investigation into any topic one chooses is assumed. Freedom of communication for the purpose of mutual assistance and the furtherance of a common enterprise—the discovery of truth—is required. A selfless devotion to the preservation of standards of validity is demanded. Such an institution selects its members, in the sense that those who are by temperament and experience inclined to welcome and obey its regulative principles are inclined to drift in that direction. It has been pointed out that the scientist becomes more and more remote from the layman, and that on this account he is either resented or overestimated. His existence is, however, excused on the grounds that out of his questioning, however remote and recondite it may be, something of practical value may emerge. He may, as perhaps is the case in this country, borrow some of the prestige of the learned man, who is often, after all, a gentleman, and used to be a gentleman of leisure.

Now this ethos is the product of a particular social situation, the product of capitalism. Of course, as we have seen, all societies must have some knowledge of how to control and exploit Nature; all societies will therefore have their technicians, and in the future they

---

[1] *Social Theory and Social Structure*, by R. K. Merton, p. 408.

will have to have specialists in those fundamental sciences which the technician employs. Whether the atmosphere of free research will be preserved, it is impossible to say. Research into human genetics was scarcely free under the Nazi régime. In these atomic days the physical sciences may preserve their freedom, though not their freedom of communication. The question here is whether *any* limitation of freedom will alter the general climate of scientific inquiry, so as to select a different type of person as scientist. When one comes to the social sciences one can see at once that they are in a precarious position. They are concerned with materials which belong to the province of evaluation in a way that the physical world does not. If a régime were established which knew all the answers to social problems, and which cared but little about how individual people were faring, what place would there be for the social scientist ? Here we are concerned with investigating friction in industry, friction on housing estates, friction in the home, and so on. If a régime were established the assumption of which was that once a certain economic change was made, then all these frictions would disappear, then the social scientist would be either otiose or intolerable. I was struck by this in China. In a conversation with two Chinese psychologists, I asked whether they were going to investigate the effects of bringing children up in institutions, which seemed to be the fashion among Chinese intellectuals, whose wives were working and who lived in small apartments. My question at first aroused suspicion. " You assume," they said, " that it will prove disastrous." " Not at all," I said, " only, it has not been found satisfactory in England, and it would be interesting to know whether it was going to be a success here." They had both been to Europe and America, so they saw the point of my question, but they clearly thought it was rather a foolish one. The emancipation of women meant that children must be brought up outside the home, and that was that. The inquiring spirit was absent.

The peculiar nature of the institutionalization of science in the régime with which we are familiar is indicated by contrast if one reads the " Report of the Scientific Session of the Academy of Sciences and the Academy of Medical Sciences of the USSR on the Physiological Teachings of Pavlov," [1] to which I have already referred. The Report contains the addresses to the Conference given by Vavilov, President of the Academy of Sciences, and by Razenov, Vice-President of the Academy of Medical Sciences. Then there are two long speeches on the development of the ideas of Pavlov by academician Bykov and academician Ivanov-Smolensky; these are followed, in the English edition, by the replies of these two academicians to the discussion, and the resolution passed by the Conference. The Report opens with an address to Stalin, in which we read: " Following your great example and your behests, we are fully aware that I. P. Pavlov's teaching is not a petrified doctrine, that it provides a scientific basis for the creative development of physiology, medicine, and psychology, of rational dietetics, physical culture and spa therapy, making for the improvement of the physical well-being of the Soviet citizen " (p. 6).

The addresses by the academicians Bykov and Ivanov-Smolensky outline the progress of physiological research, based on Pavlov's work, and the possibilities of future development. But the meeting was summoned, not for the reading of papers in general, in which various opinions might be put forward; it was called because, as Vavilov put it, " the time has come to sound the alarm " (p. 14). Some of the physiologists, especially Orbeli, who had been director of one of the Pavlov Institutes for Research into the pathology of the higher nervous activity, had

[1] Moscow, 1952.

deviated from the pure Pavlov line. Orbeli had, for example, quoted Hering with approval, and sought to distinguish Hering's philosophy from his physiology. He had actually said that it is useful to ask a patient what he feels because then you get a clue as to his objective symptoms. This distinction between " subjective " phenomena and objective phenomena is criticized on the grounds that the language which the patient uses is really a manifestation of his " second signal system," and Pavlov wrote in 1906 that " a mixture of the subjective and objective methods of investigation is harmful " (p. 125). Furthermore, it appears that Orbeli concentrated his attention on the sympathetic part of the nervous system instead of concentrating on the higher centres. Other physiologists and psychiatrists are attacked on similar lines—i.e. for not sticking to the proper path, or for daring to criticize the doctrine of the Master. The culprits were given the right to reply, and they certainly seem to have taken full use of their opportunity, to judge from the closing speeches. Orbeli accused Bykov and Ivanov-Smolensky of advertising their own accomplishments, and we are told that " Professor Anokhin's self-criticism was not what it should have been in the interests of the fruitful advancement of Pavlov's teaching." In the end the session passed a resolution in which the defects of the deviants were summed up, and " This session," we read, " condemns the unjustified tendency of certain scientists to create their own physiological ' schools ' and thus set themselves in opposition to the general trend of Pavlov's teachings " (p. 170).

Now whether one likes it or not, I suggest that the atmosphere in which physiology is carried on in the USSR, if this report is anything to go by, is very different from the atmosphere in this country. And this strangeness is further borne in upon one when one reads academician Bykov's remarks, apropos of Orbeli's misguided flirtations: "To this day we have not realized as fully as we should that effective promotion and propaganda of Pavlov's teachings is a very important sector of the ideological struggle. Only this can explain the fact that we have not subjected the reactionary opinions of foreign scientists and pseudo-scientists to trenchant, militant partisan criticism" (p. 156).

In the cognitive field, then, it has been held: (1) that certain cognitive systems are what they are because they correspond to certain structural features of the social system in which they are found; (2) the whole cognitive field tends to cohere, there is a "strain to consistency," as Parsons puts it; and (3) the topics and mode of investigation are related to socio-economic needs and to social assumptions.

In the field of evaluation, which is of course inseparable from the cognitive field since one cannot hold values in a vacuum, much the same relations between a set of values and principles and other social features can be detected. The relation between a set of values and a social structure is, however, more direct. A social structure *involves* a set of values. A kinship system *is* a system of interrelated positions with their *appropriate* roles, that is to say, roles with certain *approved* behaviour attached to them; feudalism has its inherent standards which make it what it is, and capitalism has its appropriate standards. Thus the values appropriate to a system are embedded in the system itself. So far as consistency goes we may again refer to Weber's theory of incompatibility between the standards of capitalism and those of Confucianism, Indian mysticism, and Jewish ritualism. Again, it may be the case that the capitalist emphasis on individual initiative is responsible for a heightened respect for individual privacy among the middle classes. There is, however, a rather different problem of consistency in morality, not a problem of compatibility between one evaluative system and another, but rather a problem of internal consistency. If regard for others is an accompaniment of social inter-action, if, as Homans says, interaction breeds liking, then we may have here an interactional basis for the broadening of the scope of morality. I do not think that interaction alone accounts for it, but I think it may be a condition of it. In the first place, when interaction is confined to a small group—a tribe, separated from other tribes—it may well be that moral obligations are confined within it, and this, indeed, appears to be the case. Strangers are not interactive partners, and therefore do not come within the scope of moral obligations. When, however, intermarriage or commerce brings social systems into contact with one another, the position is different. Tribal restriction breaks down, and humani-tarianism—taking account of humans as such—is on the way. I think a case could be made out to the effect that there has been a gradual, though not uninterrupted, broadening of the range over which moral obligation is thought to hold, from tribal inclusiveness to the present day. But besides increased range of interaction as a factor, I think one has to allow some place to reflection, and to the heightened moral sensitivity of particular persons. Interaction in the direct sense is obviously very limited; groups of individuals come into direct contact with groups of foreigners, and behave decently to them. But on reflection, and to those who are specially sensitive, the question is posed: If we must behave decently to these few foreigners, why not to all foreigners, why not to everyone? Hostility, greed, competition, jealousy, and so on, all operate to set bounds to the range of our obligations, but with increased indirect interaction, and with more reflection it becomes harder and harder to justify hostility and exploitation. Picking and choosing those towards whom you owe obligation is inconsistent with morality. Of course this has been said by Myrdal in his analysis of the American Dilemma, but it seems to me to have wider implications. Part of the uneasiness in the capitalist world is, I believe, due to difficulties of moral justification.

When we come to the content of moral codes, apart from those values inherent in the social system itself, and its relation to other social features, we open up a vast field of inquiry. Changes in the cognitive field obviously tend to change the relevance of certain moral precepts. As Ginsberg has shown, a great deal of the variety in moral codes is due to varieties of belief. Again, economic security enables a society to care for the sick and aged in a way which would be impossible in a society in which no unproductive member, other than children, could be supported.

One of the most obvious fields in which one can study the way different social contexts present different moral problems is the field of comparative law. Dr A. S. Diamond [1] has made a study of primitive and early civilized codes, and has found remarkable correspondence between them. Increase of material goods provides the opportunity for theft, the development of commerce raises the problem of contract, and so on. The topics with which the law is concerned vary as the ways in which people interact vary. This is obvious enough, but what is interesting is to note that there is a similarity in legal codes corresponding to the similarity of socio-economic structures. Thus there is a similarity between the law of the Franks between A.D. 500 and 814, and the law in England between A.D. 597 and 900, and the law among the Nzami people of South Africa today. Again, a comparison is drawn between the legal codes of France in A.D. 1000–1250, England A.D. 1100–1300, Assyria 1400 B.C., Hammurabi 2000 B.C., and modern Abyssinia.

Dr Diamond deals with the past. The present is the

[1] *Evolution of Law and Order* (Watts, 1951).

subject matter of Professor Friedmann's book *Law and Social Change*.[1] There he shows how large-scale monopolistic enterprises have changed the nature of contract by employing a standardized form which the customer has to accept, or forgo the service offered; he shows how the concept of liability has been extended so as to develop into " a general broad principle of legal responsibility towards the public flowing from the control of property " (p. 25), and how the increase in the scope of State activity has raised the problem of the liability of the Crown, now acknowledged by the British Crown Proceedings Act of 1947. We have in the law, as Engels observed, an " independent sphere " with its own internal consistency to preserve, but within that consistency change is always taking place in response to changes in the estimation of justice. There is scarcely a more instructive spectacle for the student of the sociology of thought than that of Judges coping with new problems in terms of concepts derived from a very different set of circumstances.

Now, in all that I have said there is what might be called a somewhat static approach. Systems of thought are taken and related to the social structure, or to other systems of thought with which they must cohere. One age or society is compared with another, we note new problems or opportunities, and point to new ideas or new laws. We have not mentioned the field of social interaction with which the word ideology is most clearly associated, the field of political conflict.

A social system is a dynamic process, not a static form. It is operated in terms of an ever-changing system of beliefs and values. Here and there we detect social systems in which the dominant features of the beliefs and values remain constant over a considerable period—or seem, from the knowledge we have of them, to remain constant. And then we see that a change has

[1] Stevens, 1951.

occurred: capitalism has taken the place of feudalism, or, in our own day, socialism has become a force to be reckoned with. The basic causes of such changes are, we are told, new technological developments and the consequential changes in the relation of production. But any given system provides its participants with certain rewards, otherwise it would not continue. Those who are in the most rewarding position will seek to preserve it, and those who find their activities hampered so that the rewards they see to be possible are unattainable, and those who believe that the rewards are inequitably divided, will seek to overthrow it. Each party will view the social scene from its own perspective, and each will develop a system of ideas congenial to its own interests. The system of ideas in terms of which the class attitudes are first formulated will be taken from the system prevailing at the time when the change begins. In his *Socialism : Utopia and Scientific*,[1] Engels points out that in its early days the struggle against feudalism " had to take on a religious disguise," though I doubt whether the word " disguise " is appropriate. As time goes on new meanings are given to old ideas, the concept of " freedom " changes its complexion, and as the struggle gets more intense the ideas of the attacking party will tend to become more extreme in opposition to the defenders of the *status quo*.

Such an account, however, is far too simple. It makes the protagonists too conscious of what we are saying they are up to. If we are to form a model of the ideal type of feudal system, before the advent of any group that could be called the *bourgeoisie*, we have, I think, to conceive of everyone accepting their position as " right." Then, unforeseeable from the point of view of feudalism, come the merchants. They are hampered, but not merely in the crude sense that they cannot satisfy their individual

[1] p. 95.

interests; they cannot do the job of doing business effectively. What one might call the logic of their occupation demands a new order.

The rise of socialism is, I think, somewhat different because moral issues are more obviously involved. However, there is a sense in which the two cases are similar. According to the Marxists, private enterprise and its successor, the joint-stock company, have carried the methods of production to their limits under existing productive relations, but now—and indeed for some time —what I have ventured to call the " occupational logic " leads to one crisis after another, so that production, rather than being helped, is hindered. Only if the producers themselves take over will production go forward to further heights. What might be called " the logic of production " demands it. On the other side the view is expressed that only a competitive system is efficient and that the progress in Russia and China is due to the fact that they are backward countries. On this view the " logic of production " demands competition.

Now in these two very simplified cases we have not only an historical, but a theoretical problem. If social systems are boundary-maintaining systems, as Parsons expresses it, which means that it is sensible to talk of equilibrating mechanism, then when a disturbance occurs, as in the case of the rise of the *bourgeoisie* in the feudal system and the rise of the working-class movement in the capitalist system, we ought to be able to make certain predictions. We can say, for instance, that the representatives of the régime under attack will resist. But can we go beyond such trivialities ? The problem is focused in two passages from Engels' *Socialism : Utopia and Scientific*. In one passage he says: " The growing perception that existing social institutions are unreasonable and unjust . . . is only *proof* that in the modes of production and exchange changes have silently taken place with which the social order, adapted to earlier economic conditions, is no longer in keeping." [1] In a previous passage, dealing with Robert Owen, he says: " The new mode of production was, as yet, only at the beginning of its period of ascent; as yet it was the normal, regular method of production—the only one possible under existing conditions." Then he goes on to say that Robert Owen was horrified. Now there is a slight inconsistency here, I think. Owen perceived injustice when the régime was the only possible one, and therefore *not* breaking down. However, the point is that Owen failed. Utopias, in Engel's sense, may be proclaimed, but they remain Utopias until the time is ripe for change, and then something more realistic, or " scientific " as Engels would say, will be the form in which the representatives of the rising party will express themselves. The theoretical question is: can we, by the application of some principle of equilibrium, detect the moment when the strains in the system are such that it is bound to break down? I doubt whether we can. Certain general expectations we can have, to be sure. We can, perhaps, presume that employers would try to improve factory conditions and social relations in industry; not merely to safeguard their personal interests, but as functionaries of a disturbed system. We can expect the attackers to say that they are merely keeping the working class quiet: holidays with pay are a more effective opium than that purveyed by the ministers of religion. Or we might see, as Lenin did in 1902, when contemplating the Russian situation, that spontaneous action on the part of the proletariat, unguided by socialist intellectuals, would lead them into the socially safe channels of trade unionism, which is just what the system requires for its preservation. Past moves and present tactics we can explain in this way, but the future is, as I have suggested, impenetrable.

[1] p. 125.

Mannheim, if I understand him rightly, would have agreed. In that part of his *Ideology and Utopia* in which he discusses the " prospects of scientific politics," he contrasts intellectualistic science with dynamic synthesis. Admittedly he was more interested in educating politicians than in teaching sociology; but he calls our attention to the obvious and distressing fact that the practical man of affairs nearly always knows more about social affairs than does the sociologist, whose business it is to study them. " When," he says, " we enter the realm of politics, in which everything is in process of becoming and when the collective element in us, as knowing subjects, helps to shape the process of becoming, when thought is not contemplative from the point of view of a spectator, but rather the active participation and reshaping of the process itself, a new type of knowledge seems to emerge. . . . In these realms there is no such thing as a purely theoretical outlook on the part of the observer." [1]   There is clearly something in this. We may argue that participants, particularly if they are an attacking party, are more sensitive to what is going on than are outside observers. We may also agree that in some sense we know about people and their motives in a way we cannot know about physical objects. There is not, however, a new kind of knowledge in politics. Our theories about other people and groups of people are as theoretical as are our theories about natural science.

However, whether you call it a new kind of knowledge or not, there is much to be said for the view that knowledge about the way in which people's political ideas and policies are shaped by their position in the struggle can best be acquired by those actively engaged in it. That, surely, is why the writings of Marx, Engels, and Lenin are so illuminating. The active deviant group is

[1] Kegan Paul, 1936, p. 152.

likely to have a greater awareness of the part they are
playing; the *status quo* party—if one can call them such—
have not only to preserve their interests, but their reputa-
tions as well, by expressing themselves in terms of the
morality agreed upon by both. This means that the
defence is often less aware of what is going on than is
the attacking force.

Finally, I must touch upon a problem which has
concerned writers about the sociology of knowledge, a
problem which lands us in the forests of philosophical
disputation. This is a region in which I, a mere student
of sociology, fear to tread; I so easily lose my way.
The problem is, simply stated: If knowledge is socially
conditioned, does this not impugn its validity? It is a
problem for those who think of reality or truth as something absolute to which in our thinkings and arguings
we can approximate or even reach. "If," they say,
"our beliefs are conditioned by the social structure in
which we participate, what guarantee can we possibly
have that any of these are true?" I have already said
that I think that a great deal of thinking is not socially
conditioned in the sense that if we knew the social
system in which it occurred we could predict the thoughts.
This, however, does not dispose of the difficulty. It
seems to me that the problem ought to be tackled from
the point of view of the social conditioning of knowledge
itself. Systems of belief and value are developed and
preserved by and in human intercourse. Our cognitive
discourse is carried on in terms of reality, our beliefs
are in terms of reality. When, however, we consider
the *validity* or *acceptability* of our beliefs and theories, we
are bound by mutually accepted standards. There is,
so far as I can see, nothing else. There is no peep behind
the scenes. When we ask whether the belief is valid,
we rely for our answer on whatever kind of argument is
mutually accepted as convincing. In our system we

apply the general rules of scientific evidence because this is the agreed standard. In another system it might be agreed to abide by the reply of an oracle. We should say that such a procedure is silly, and so it is—from the point of view of the scientific standard; but then the oracle is not "in on" the scientific act. What I am saying is that our belief systems themselves are social products and that the validity of their components is determined by standards which are also social products. There may, of course, be sudden revelations such as those described by William James as being vouchsafed under the influence of nitrous oxide when "depth upon depth of truth seems revealed to the inhaler." [1] When, however, a belief is justified or argued about, the holder of the belief must appeal to standards which are acceptable to the person or group to whom he is addressing himself. His hypothesis is acceptable if it fits the standards; if not, not. There will, of course, be different estimates of validity or acceptability, from group to group, and from person to person. One group's frame of reference may differ from that of another; there may be differences of opinion about the appropriate standards to apply, and even if the standards are agreed upon, there may be differences of opinion as to how far the evidence brought forward supports the proposition under consideration. The emotional appeal of a belief may weigh more with its holder, without his being aware of the fact, than does the standard which is being applied to it. All the same, when he tries to defend it he is appealing to agreed standards. He may appeal to authority, he may appeal to logic, he may appeal to verification, or he may appeal to what is vaguely called "our understanding of human nature." These are socially engendered standards in the sense that they would not exist if society did not exist. If he can find no one to accept the particular standard

[1] *Varieties of Religious Experience* (Longmans, 1922), p. 387.

he wishes to apply to a particular hypothesis, then it may remain valid for him, and for no one else. If he persuades a group that a belief fits the standards which they agree to be appropriate, then it is valid for them. To look for some absolute validity, is to look for universal agreement. Only in terms of agreement and disagreement between persons is there any sense in the notion " validity," that I can see. And if it be said that this theory itself is a social product, I at once agree. Furthermore, I have to confess that you may, by applying mutually agreed standards, show me that I am wrong.

Index